THE BRIDLEWAYS OF BRITAIN

Edited by Annabel Whittet
with contributions from Pamela D. Stewart

WHITTET BOOKS

First published 1986

© 1986 by Annabel Whittet

Maps © 1986 by Whittet Books
Whittet Books Ltd, 18 Anley Road, London W14 0BY

Design by Richard Kelly
Maps by David J. Stevens

The information in this book is given in good faith and is correct
at the time of going to press, as far as can be ascertained.

British Library Cataloguing in Publication Data

The Bridleways of Britain.
  1. Trails—Great Britain—Guide-books
  2. Great Britain—Description and travel—971–
  —Guide-books
  I. Whittet, Annabel
  914.1'04858   DA632

ISBN 0–905483–49–9
ISBN 0–905483–48–0 Pbk

Typeset by Inforum Ltd, Portsmouth
Printed and bound by Oxford University Press

Contents

Acknowledgments

Many people have given their time to help on this book, and in particular I would like to thank Pamela D. Stewart, Sam and Sylvia Hart and Mrs Edith Boon for their most generous help. Others I wish to thank are: Charles Shippam, Pat Kingston, Pauline Cutler, Margery Price, Nancy Hay, the Horse and Pony Endurance Society of Great Britain, Mrs Anne Mortley, Mrs Ann Fraser, Donald Pearse, Lady Miranda Emmet, Aza Pinney, Mrs K. H. Widdup, Hilary Kristensen, Lt Col. R.C. Yule, O.B.E., the Ancient Order of Packriders, Mrs L.M.K. Gibbins, Edith Whetham, R.W. Looker, Mrs R.H.N. Worsley, Mrs Ruth Colyer, Dr Phyllis Croft, Sheila Beardall, Anne Lee, Diana Roberts, The Exeter Area Bridleways Association, Shipton Riding Club, Paul Plaster, Andrew Chitty, Reginald Bishop, Katharine Hands, A.C. Jones, Norman K. Brown, Celia Greasley, Lys Pilcher, Mrs V. Jeffries, Roland P. Lay, Masie Portlock, Gudrun Webb, Mrs Jane Nicholson, John A.L. Carter, Mrs S.W. Ashenden-Bax, Vicky Robinson, Janet M. Boulton, Mrs Pamela Gormley, Miss P.L. Cook, Mrs H. Johns, Diana Lee, Mike Russell, Miss V.A. Waistell, M.W. Smith, Glen Hood, Maurice Edden, Mrs R.C. Eld, Mrs B. Dean, Mrs Jane Cox, Terence Bowden, David and Janice Lewardowski and Keith Abell.

Foreword

Long distance riding is a fast growing, competitive sport and a source of pleasure to many, but riding long distances is also the treasured recreation of a considerable number of riders who love to cover miles of glorious British countryside at their leisure, enjoying the companionship of their great friend, the horse.

This simple aim may sound easy to achieve, but is far from being so. The spread of urbanism with its outlying industrial estates and accompanying fast, heavy traffic, intensive farming and obstructed rights of way on what is left of the countryside all combine to cause even the short distance riders to fear for their lives each time they venture outside their field or stable. That it is still possible to find some safe places to ride, particularly over long stretches of beautiful scenery, is mainly due to a band of devoted enthusiasts who have spent long hours finding, linking or negotiating suitable routes for others to use in the future.

In this book is a selection of some of the results of their labours, and it is hoped that many readers will be able to enjoy them.

However, this is not really the end of the story. It should be an ongoing saga which concerns every horse-owner, or parent of pony-owning children, towards the care and preservation of those byways, green lanes and bridleways that still remain to us, and in the quest for old routes which should have been incorporated into the available network – but were not.

It seems incredible that, up to about fifty years ago, motor vehicles were comparatively scarce in number, and horses still widely in use for transport, haulage and agriculture. Middle aged people at that time could clearly remember the whereabouts of the traditional bridleways from former times, when the horse was the generally used and only alternative to the pedalcycle or walking; one needed to be pretty wealthy to own a motor car before 1930. It was only in the next decade that cars and lorries swelled steadily in numbers, and the outbreak of World War II provoked an explosion not only of motor traffic but of military camps, aerodromes and intensive farming. Riding, in comparison, shrank as the younger generation left home on active service while the older folk were otherwise occupied on the home front.

Age-old rights of way were closed under Emergency Orders, ploughed out or otherwise obstructed without protest from the public; a process carried on after 1946 to such an extent that, by 1949, even the government of the day took belated alarm and tried to remedy the situation by introducing appropriate legislation. The result was the 'National Parks and Access to the Countryside Act, 1949'. This, among other things, ordered each County Council to instruct each Parish Council in its area to list every right of way in that parish under three headings: (a) 'Road used as a public path' or RUPP (which probably once had carriage rights but was now mainly used for walking or riding), (b) bridleway or (c) footpath.

After consultation and collation, the County Council was responsible for the production of a 'Definitive Map' which showed the whereabouts and status of every right of way in the county, plus a written 'statement' describing the route of the way; any right shown on the map was conclusive evidence that it existed at the time the map was published. One could legally walk or ride (or lead) a horse on a RUPP, and possibly take a vehicle along it, walk and ride (or lead) a horse along a bridleway, and walk only on a footpath unless the landowner had given permission to do otherwise.

County Councils, the (then) Rural District Councils and Parish Councils were all to keep copies of the Definitive Map relevant to their own particular area and hold it available for the general public to see on demand, and this is still so at the present date. However, there may have been various legally permitted reasons why the original map has been slightly altered since 1949 to deal with additions, deletions or changes in the line of a route; most counties have probably published a new, up-to-date Definitive Map by now since the coming into force of the Wildlife and Countryside Act, 1981.

Some of the more recent Ordnance Survey maps show rights of way which may not now be accurate or up to date, so every rider should make the effort to see, and perhaps copy onto their own map, what rights of way are registered on the current Definitive Map in order to be certain of their facts.

It is useful to know a few facts about the law regarding the use of rights of way, and very surprising to find out how much of the law is in the user's favour. A brief resumé on this subject appears at the end of this book, together with a bibliography and list of useful addresses.

Happy Riding!

January 1986   *Pamela D. Stewart*

Introduction

As a non-competitive rider who enjoys the countryside from a horse's back, I decided to compile this book because of the frustration I experienced trying to find new and long riding routes. I would scrutinize the Ordnance Survey map, pinpoint a lovely line of long red (or, now, green) dashes and ride to it, only to be baulked by a padlocked gate, barbed wire across the track, streams with no bridges and crops growing high over the indicated bridleway. No matter how well you check out the rights of way (as will be fully explained by Pamela Stewart in Law and Lore on Rights of Way, p. 171) this is no guarantee that the way will be accessible. Nor that your way will not be blocked by an irate landowner who, despite your waving the OS map in his face, persists that it is his land, and orders you off it. We can all help in the campaign to rescue bridleways from obstruction and extinction (again, see Pamela Stewart) and let us hope that bodies like the Countryside Commission will recognize the need for places for people to ride as well as to walk in order not only to provide a leisure requirement but also to prevent road accidents involving horses. At the moment, sadly, the long distance paths designated by the Countryside Commission (and they are excellent) do not for the most part cater for riders. Only one of them (the Ridgeway) is a bridlepath for its entire length.

This book aims to give you the best riding routes in the country without your having to check out their rideability; all of them have been checked. They take you over glorious countryside, high in the Pennines, into the Cheviots, over Salisbury Plain, the mountains of Wales and to the North Norfolk coast. They lead you past ancient monuments like Stonehenge, Avebury, Wayland's Smithy, Silbury Hill, Offa's Dyke, Cerne Abbas Giant and several white horses, as well as places of modern interest such as Watership Down and into the town of Haworth, home of the Brontes. Sometimes you may be riding down ancient tracks like the Ridgeway or the Peddar's Way, old coach roads now overgrown and forgotten, like the Salisbury to Marlborough road or perhaps on more modern paths made out of disused railway lines. All of them aim to keep you off the roads as far as possible. I am extremely grateful to all those who contributed routes and helped me in my lengthy enquiries for the book. During the course of my research I met many enthusiasts who take two and three week trips on their horses, carrying their possessions with them; one of them rode unshod! Apart from these enthusiasts, more and more people are re-discovering the delights of long-distance riding – for pleasure and for sport. Events like the Golden Horseshoe Ride have stimulated interest, and other associations such as the Horse and Pony Endurance Society organize events over long distances. The rides in the book vary in length from eighteen to two hundred miles and can offer either a good holiday or a day ride.

The worst part of preparing for a long ride is mapping your route – with this book that task should be removed. However, you still must plan your days' journeys and overnight accommodation for horse and rider – unless you have good contacts in the area, it can be difficult to achieve close proximity. Don't forget that without your horse you have lost your transport; you probably will not feel like walking miles with your belongings to your bed and breakfast. And bear in mind that you have to get supper close at hand. Wherever possible I have given hints on people who may help with stabling and grazing in connection with specific routes. Other sources of information are: the British Horse Society's booklet *Bed and Breakfast for Horses: Stabling and Grazing* (see Bibliography); the British Horse Society also publishes a list of approved riding stables, which will often allow you to rent a stable for the night and sell you some feed. Failing these, try non-listed riding stables in the area, or helpful farmers. But do make sure you check the price of stabling/grazing *and* an evening and morning feed before booking; we once thought we were being charged £5 per horse for a night (reasonable) and then were told in the morning that the feed was another £5 per horse – more expensive than the human accommodation.

The fitness of your horse and the total length of your ride will partly determine your daily mileage (and of course the proximity of places to stay); we do 25–30 miles a day, with rest days every 3 or 4 days. This works out, taking into account wasting time getting lost, cutting barbed wire fences, opening gates, finding water troughs and diversions to look at the odd church, at about 6 hours riding.

You don't want to be laden down like a packhorse so that at every gallop your saddlebags, macintosh, shoes tied on with bits of string and concertina maps flap and wallop in all directions. We use old Air Force kitbags, which were originally sewn with tapes, but we discovered were much better tightly tied with string all round to form a rigid sausage, which we then attach to the front D rings of the saddle. The tightness ensures that the bundle won't bounce around too much. Weight distribution is also important – obviously it should be even either side, but the greatest weight should be in the middle, again to prevent flapping. I wouldn't recommend attaching anything to yourself, because you will, after a while, find it very uncomfortable. If you're affluent, you can get hand-made leather saddle bags which fit to the back of the saddle and the girth. A trekking numnah, which has two small pockets rather insecurely fastened, is excellent for light items, such as maps, but hopeless for anything heavy, as I found to my cost at the end of a gallop across a hayfield, when I had to retrace my steps, poking in the drying hay to find two rather expensive sandals, a hoofpick, a dandy brush and a penknife. For those who can't spend a weekend without a large suitcase, packing can be difficult.

The most essential piece of equipment is your map (and/or copy of this book, preferably both); the maps referred to in the book are OS 1:50,000 pink ones. The 1:25,000 series indicates bridleways better, but if travelling any distance you'd need a trailer to carry all the maps. Next you'll need a plastic folder to keep maps dry when it's raining; lots of bits of baler twine; a hoofpick; penknife; compass; wire-cutters; if staying with non-horsey people, a brush. Keeping a headcollar on under the bridle is convenient when you stop for lunch or a drink; carry long pieces of strong rope to attach to the headcollar rope and then in turn to a piece of baler twine, and, as long as you fix to a heavy object and your horse is sensible, you can leave it to graze whilst you eat your sandwiches. (Speaking of which, carrying sandwiches in your numnah is a recipe for breadcrumbs and flakes of butter coating the inside of the pouch rather than a recipe for a tasty lunch.) Water for horses can be a problem, though many publicans will oblige with a bucket (can be embarrassing when your horse, supposedly exhausted and thirsty after a hefty journey, sniffs the bucket and rejects the offering). Someone wrote that water troughs were only available over fences, and she resorted to scooping water up in her riding hat. Putting two numnahs under the saddle has the advantages of both giving the horse more protective padding and enabling you to rotate the clean and the dirty one if you don't have time to wash them.

One last warning: if you are staying with people who don't own horses, you may have a problem with feed. On one occasion I sent what my host referred to as 'the horse sandwiches' through the post in advance in a large box. Others I have met have asked their hosts to get 'some oats' and been presented with porridge oats, at which their horse turned its nose. To expect a horse to do 30 miles a day without a short feed seems to me rather a tall order.

I hope that the book will give you a lot of pleasure and encourage the provision of facilities for long distance riders. I would love to hear from peole who have suggestions of good routes. Many many thanks to all those who spent time helping me research the book and who provided routes. Names of contributors of routes used in the book are given under the titles of each route; but sadly I was sent lots that I could not use in this book (maybe in the next one).

The Routes

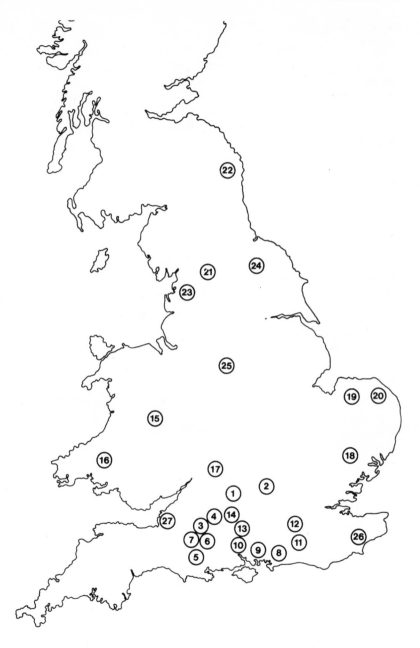

A note on the maps

The maps are orientated north to the top of the page. They are sketch maps only, not accurate as to scale, and based on personal observation. They will enable you to pick out your route, and the text gives National Grid References, but we strongly recommend that you also buy the relevant OS 1:50,000 mpa. When routes continue over more than one map letters A, B, C, etc, indicate where they recommence on the next map.

KEY

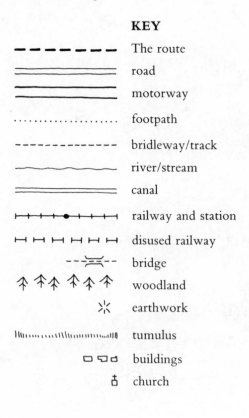

— — — — —	The route
═══════	road
▬▬▬▬▬	motorway
....	footpath
- - - - - - -	bridleway/track
～～～～～	river/stream
════════	canal
⊢+⊢+•+⊢+⊣	railway and station
⊢⊣ ⊢⊣ ⊢⊣ ⊢⊣ ⊢⊣	disused railway
--⟨≡⟩--	bridge
🌲 🌲🌲 🌲🌲 🌲	woodland
⋇	earthwork
ⅠⅠⅠⅠ.....⊥⊥⊥⊥⊥......⊥⊥	tumulus
▢ ▽◁	buildings
⌂	church

1 The Ridgeway Path

with the help of
Pamela D. Stewart

Approx. 69k, 43 miles

OS maps 173,174

Start: 103700:OS 173
Finish: 589815:OS 174

The Countryside Commission path is open from Avebury to Streatley to horses, and is a broad track with some of the best turf in the country high on the downs with views north and south. The path is well marked with the Countryside Commission acorn signs and should present no problem, except perhaps in accommodation and water.

The Countryside Commission route, though it differs from the original route, still passes near fascinating historical sites, Iron Age hill forts and white horses, Avebury stone circle, and in the vicinity of Silbury Hill and West Kennet Long Barrow. The original Ridgeway (still marked on Ordnance Survey maps), which is older than Avebury (built approx. 2000–1600 BC), was a network of upland paths: they were high on the hills in order to avoid the thick woods and undergrowth lower down. The track was for man and animals, but it was a kind of ancient bypass – it didn't lead to villages, which would mostly have been in the valleys. To solve the water problem were dewponds, shallow indentations in the downs where water is reputed to have gathered; sadly, the dewponds don't provide modern travellers with any moisture, though you can occasionally see them by the path.

Avebury, where you join the Ridgeway route on OS173, was a massive stone circle, parts of which still stand. The Great Stone Circle was a megalithic masterpiece, whose purpose is still unknown, though it has astronomical significance. Undoubtedly it was a meeting place and a site for ceremonies. It was connected to the Sanctuary (near the beginning of the Ridgeway by the A4) by a stone avenue. The great stone circle was originally complete (in recent centuries the stones were removed to build cottages in the village) and surrounded two or three smaller circles.

Older than Avebury, which was built by Bronze Age peoples, are the long barrows such as West Kennet and Wayland's Smithy, which were built by neolithic men. After the Beaker people in the Bronze Age came the Celts, who farmed using rectangular fields; they dug ditches, such as Grim's Ditch, and Barbury, Liddington, Uffington and Segsbury castles, to defeat the new wave of Celts coming in the Iron Age. This theory is disputed by J.R.L. Anderson (in *The Oldest Road*, Wildwood House, 1975) who reckons that the forts were sited against attack from the north and attributes them to the 'Beaker People' prior to 1000 BC.

We join the Ridgeway path just east of Avebury (135708), turning left and proceeding north, doing a dog-leg east and then back north, crossing Hackpen Hill and the minor road from Broad Hinton to Marlborough, where there is space for parking. Hackpen white horse lies below the Ridgeway but cannot be seen; it is not ancient, but was cut in 1838. Continue for another couple of miles till you meet minor road from Wrough-

ton (145764) where the Countryside Commission diverts from the old Ridgeway path and you should turn right onto the road and then left, going through a couple of bridle gates uphill and on to Barbury Castle, an Iron Age hill fort, thought to date from about 500 BC. It is not a castle in the usual sense of the word, but a defensive earthwork, still impressive, with a deep circular ditch and flat central area, high on the downs, with views over the Ray valley to the north.

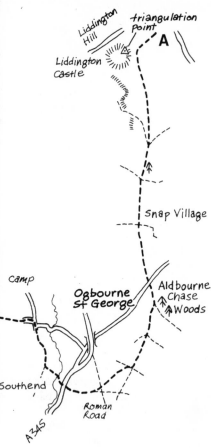

Smeathe's Ridge, a lovely section of grassy path with splendid views, before descending beside old thorn bushes (typical of an old road) through another gate to Smeathe's Plantation and a chalky path where on the left they are destroying the old army encampment. Join the minor road for a short distance, turning right, and, at the next bend, go straight ahead (signposted) between high hedges. Although this grassy track leads to Ogbourne St Andrew, you turn left, downhill towards Southend and rejoin a metalled road which crosses the A345 (and onto map 174).

Follow the signposted track, under railway bridge, across ancient Roman Road, and onto another track (briefly right, and then left) down a rather overgrown path to meet up with another, veering north, passing Aldbourne Chase Woods and joining a metal road to cross minor road Albourne to Ogbourne St George (214754). Straight over here (parking possible at this junction) following the track beside a field and into a lane, closely overgrown with bushes and trees, and full of flies in summer. Over another two tracks and the path forks left towards Liddington Hill, leaving it to the north where stands another Iron Age castle. The Ridgeway passes to the east of the castle, but if you were to go up to it (difficult on a horse), you

Go straight through the castle, through another bridle gate and on to a very large car park, with another bridle gate, and also a ladies' and gentlemen's convenience. The bridle path carries on to the right of the car park, joins the minor road briefly (turning right) and then the path is entered again through a bridle gate to the left (signposted). This leads you to

would find a triangulation post erected 'Liddington Hill, the hill beloved of Richard Jefferies and Alfred Williams'. (Jefferies, 1848–87, was the renowned naturalist and author, who was born at Coate and wrote about the West Country. Alfred Williams, 1877–1930, was a local poet.) Passing through the fields, the track comes out through a gate onto a stony lane and to the A419. Here you must turn left, and it would be best to keep to the verge on the left until you reach the signs pointing down the minor road to the east,

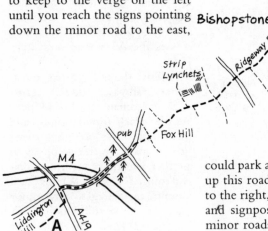

could park a box. A short distance up this road, the Ridgeway turns to the right, with a small car park and signpost. You cross various minor roads, and to your left are strip lynchets, raised terraces, which you can't actually get to from the Ridgeway.

Having crossed the surfaced road leading from Bishopstone (253827) the path goes north, passes a gate and becomes narrower than the usual broad track, and confined between bushes. Having crossed the minor road B4000 (where there's room to park beside the road), the track

which carries you over the M4 (slightly alarming for horses) and into Fox Hill, a small village with the honour of having the only pub on the Ridgeway Path, the Shepherd's Rest (they are well used to walkers, with notices dissuading muddy boots, and fairly well used to horse travellers). There's a good broad grass verge where you

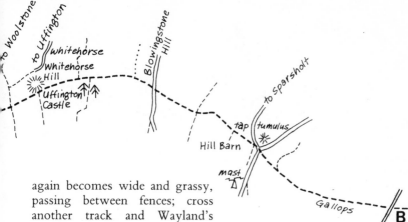

again becomes wide and grassy, passing between fences; cross another track and Wayland's Smithy lies to the left of the track, some 50 yards from it and in a little wood. It is a megalithic tomb (even older than West Kennet) although the name is Saxon; the myth is that if you left your horse by the tomb and put a coin on the lintel stone, you would return to find your horse shod by Wayland (the Saxon god of smithies). So if one's horse's shoes were loose, one would be tempted to try, but unfortunately you can't take a horse through the gate to the monument.) Having crossed a couple more tracks, you come to Whitehorse Hill and Uffington Castle. The going varies from broad springy turf to deeply rutted (and in wet weather flooded) path.

The Uffington White Horse, the most famous and most beautiful (almost modern in design) unfortunately cannot be seen from the Ridgeway. If you want to visit it you must divert down the track leading to Woolstone and turn right. No one knows who cut this white horse but it was probably in the 1st century BC or AD. Curiously you cannot see the shape of the horse well, even if you are in the valley beneath the Ridgeway. To the west of the horse is the so called 'Manger', a steep valley, and a flat topped hill called Dragon Hill (where St George is supposed to have slain the Dragon). To the right of the path is Uffington Castle. Gentle rolling hills take you past chalky sites full of orchids.

The next minor road you cross is Blowingstone Hill: the name comes from a sarsen stone in a cottage garden at the foot of the hill. The stone is riddled with holes and if you blow through the holes a strange sound can be emitted. The path rises to Hill Barn Clump and then declines past notable and

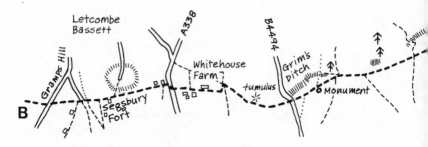

typical thorn bushes to the junction of the minor road from Sparsholt and the B4001. The broad grassy turf of the Ridgeway here is inviting enough, but beside it run gallops that are even more inviting. At Gramp's Hill a track crosses the path and several tracks around Segsbury fort, another hill fort, which you can see better by leaving the Ridgeway on the metal road. The 'fort' is enormous. The A338, a busy major road, must be joined for a short distance (turning south), until turning left (signposted to 'Mill Farm' and Ridgeway). Parking either side of this road with wide verges. Metal road as far as farm.

When you see the tumulus (long barrow) you turn left and then right and onto the B4494. Here again is space for parking. Fork right and on to Scutchamer Knob, a Saxon barrow; it is a curious hollow mound surrounded by trees. (A 'scutcher' was used to beat flax.) They used to hold fairs here. Just east of the knob a road, surfaced to the Ridgeway, leads from East

Hendred and here parking is available. More splendid turf, and gallops beside you; Grim's Ditch lies to the north – a line of prehistoric ditches, possibly defensive, but difficult to see. The A34 is a nasty busy road to cross, and you must do so at the top of a hill with bad visibility.

The way leads you south (whereas the old path goes north) to meet a concrete road; more gallops beside the path, but the way itself is good enough for you not to mind being excluded. Follow signs, and gallops, east and onto old wood shavings, an ideal riding surface.

Ignore a turning south and go downhill to cross a bridge over the railway cutting (the line is disused). The Ridgeway now climbs over Roden Downs, though an alternative route would lead you left, going due east and onto the Fair Mile, very good riding, but it comes out on the A417. If you stick on the Ridgeway, you pass a junction where are the site of a Roman-British temple and also a

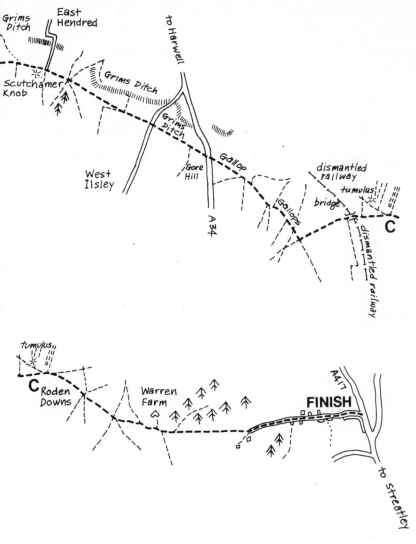

barrow. The Ridgeway again becomes hedged and narrow and descends by Warren Farm to a metal road (Rectory Road) leading into Streatley. There is parking at the junction of the track and the metal road, and indeed it might be best to be met here judging by dispirited walkers we passed trekking into suburban Streatley.

2 Goring to Ivinghoe Beacon
(the Icknield Way)

Roland P. Lay

Approx. 65k, 41 miles

OS maps 165, 175

Start: 600808:OS175

Finish: 971191:OS165

The Icknield Way passes to the north and north-west of the beacon as the B489 Tring-Dunstable road. There are no bridleways from this point, and therefore a more satisfactory end may be the village of Edlesborough about 2½ miles north-east of Beacon Hill; in any event it is mainly roadway from Ivinghoe Village to Wendover.

On leaving the Ridgeway you arrive at the road junction which leads to Warren Farm, follow the road to the right passing Thurle Grange on the left, and then right again on to the A417. At the road junction turn right onto the A329 and then left on to the B4009 at the traffic lights; this road crosses the river between Goring and Streatley and you remain on this road till you get to the minor crossroads at Kaffirs (626843), where you turn left off the road onto a track which continues for about 1½ miles. (NOTE: there is some confusion about the track at Kaffirs and it may be necessary to follow the minor road past Kaffirs to the A4074, where you turn left, and then after a short distance on the verge, turn right on minor road.)

On your left is Coblers Hill, and the track takes you through Drunken Bottom following the course of the Icknield Way. Cross the Crowmarsh road and follow the road to cross the Ridgeway Path and pass Blenheim Farm. Cross the A423 and follow the

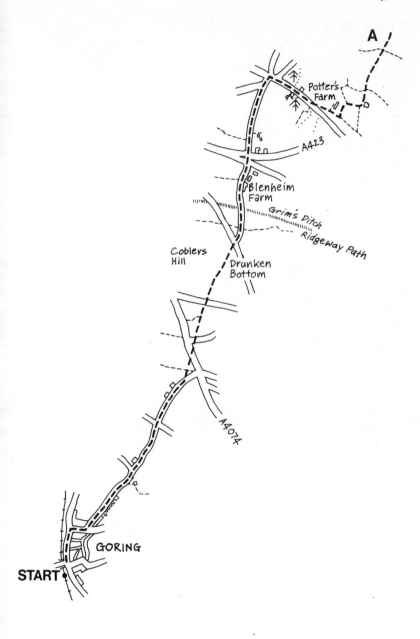

A

Potter's
Farm

A423

Blenheim
Farm

Grim's Ditch

Ridgeway Path

Coblers
Hill

Drunken
Bottom

A4074

GORING

START

roadway. (There is an alternative route, which is to follow the Ridgeway to the west in order to arrive at this point, but that would involve more roadwork, so this route is recommended.)

Continue turning right to irregular crossroads where you turn right and then fork left and then turn left up track towards Potter's Farm and then carry on northwards to Warren Farm. Down Farm will be on your left and you turn right (667913) on to a very short length of minor road. Pass North Farm and Icknieldbank Plantation on the right and continue to cross the minor Britwell to Stonor road. Cross the B480 at Icknield House and the Icknield Way crosses the Watlington-Turville road at White Mark west of Watlington Hill. Continue north-easterly along the track under the new M40 underpass and cross the A40 below Beacon Hill and the minor road at Kingston Crossing. The Icknield Way continues following the line of the old railway on the left and goes in a north-easterly direction to cross the Chinnor to Crowell road near the chalk quarries. Now you are on the Ridgeway Path, which, when you turn right, becomes the

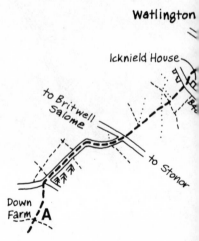

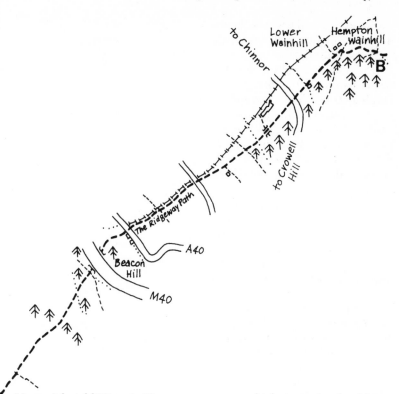

Upper Icknield Way. At Hempton Wainhill you cross the road at the Buckinghamshire/Oxfordshire boundary and continue on to the road to Bledlow which you cross and over another crossroads. Under one railway line and over another and then turn left onto the A4010, which is not too busy, for about ¼ mile.

Take the next right onto a minor road passing the outskirts of Princes Risborough on the left and crossing a minor road junction turning into a track. This bridle-way, which is again the Upper Icknield Way, brings you out at a minor road junction (818040) where you turn right for about 200 yards until the road turns sharp left; here you take the track turning right round an old chalk pit and following the perimeter of the open field. Continue along the woodside and northerly to meet an open field. The track enters the wood and then emerges to follow the edge of the wood for about ½ mile. You come out onto the road at the No Parking sign on the

tree, and turn right to pass Long-
down Farm lying in the valley on
the right. Take the track on the left
which intersects with another
track, where you turn right and
climb up through beech woods to
meet the road. Turn left on the
road and round the bend to the
right passing the main entrance
gates to Chequers on your left.
After ½ mile, after the right-hand
turning, take the track to the right
and follow for about ½ mile before
turning left and following through
the woods where two bridleways
converge. This brings you out on
the road just east of the junction
with the Butler's Cross road (immediately   opposite,   again,   is
Chequers). Up the hill, along the
good verges of the road, until the
bridleway goes straight ahead just
south-east of Coombe Hill to veer
to the north-east and onto the road
(864074) where you turn right.

Over the railway bridge, and
turn sharp right into Wendover
High Street, which is the Icknield
Way again. At the side of the Free
Church Chapel you turn left down
a small road track which will bring
you out on a minor road where
you turn right and then left after
about 300 yards down the minor
road to pass Halefield on the right.
After about a mile (881074) take
the track to the left into Forestry
Commission land. Although this
is a well marked ride, with small
white horse shoes painted on to 4"
by 4" posts driven into the ground,

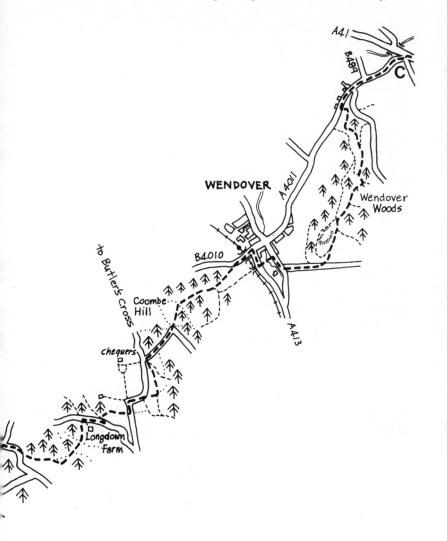

it is not a public bridleway and it may be advisable to write to the Head Forester for a permit (he is at the Forestry Commission, Upper Icknield Way, Aston Clinton, Aylesbury, Bucks). Carry on due north through Wendover Woods taking a left-hand turn at the cross-roads of tracks (888090) until you reach the A4011, which you must follow (it is not too busy except in rush-hour periods) for about 1¼ miles.

Turning right on the A4011 you continue till reaching the junction with the A41 and turn right up Tring Hill till reaching the junction with the A41 at the top of Tring Hill (this point is part of the eventual Motorway M41 but at the time of writing serves only as a bypass to Tring; it is extremely busy at rush hour periods: 8–10 a.m.; 4–6 p.m.). Turn north on the B488, which is the Upper Icknield Way (less busy than the Lower, which is parallel), for about 4 miles till the road does an abrupt wiggle to the right before crossing the railway and after a sharp left-hand bend arriving in the village of Ivinghoe. Turn left at the road junction (B489) and then right at the village road and onto a track leading north-eastwards, climbing a hill and going through a cutting to cross a minor road south-east of Ivinghoe Aston. This track brings you out at Edlesborough, Church End, the end of this route.

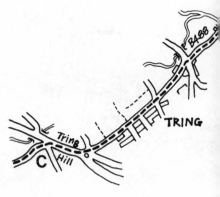

In the event that overnight provision for horse is made at Mayertorne, upon reaching the road junction from Wendover Woods, turn left handed and follow the road southwards to a track on the

Edlesborough

FINISH

Ivinghoe

windmill

to Beacon Hill

A4146 and

B4811

Grand Union Canal

continue for about 100 yards to turn right handed along a lane which is high up on the ridge giving views across the valley to the west. After nearly 1 mile, and passing a farm on the right hand, turn right handed and continue down hill at the bottom of which is a farmstead and Bowood Antiques; turn left here and follow to the main road and immediately opposite is Mayertorne Cottage.

The original route can be picked up; leaving the cottage and following the main road northwards for about ⅓ mile and then turning left handed in to a lane which will follow through beechwoods to Coblers Hill, about 1 mile, here turn left handed and follow the track along the edge of woodlands to Dunsmore, and immediately past the Black Horse turn left handed on the minor road and follow this to the junction with the minor road south-east of Coombe Hill.

Possible accommodation
Mr Roland P. Lay, Mayertorne Cottage, Wendover Dean, Aylesbury, Bucks. Tel. (0296) 622297 can provide overnight stabling if given advance notice; there is an inn ¼ mile away for riders.

left just before reaching the Wellhead Inn. Turn along the track, which is part of the Ridgeway Path, and continue for nearly 1½ miles past Concord and on to a minor roadway. Turn left and

3 The Great Ridgeway
(to connect with Ridgeway Path)

Pamela D. Stewart

Approx. 75k, 47 miles

OS maps 184, 173

Start: 894298:OS 184

Finish: 125709:OS 173

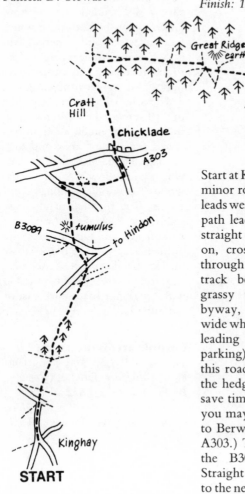

Start at Kinghay on OS 184, where minor road turns sharply. A track leads west, but due north the bridle-path leads to the edge of a field, straight through the next field and on, crossing another bridleway, through a wood (897307). This track becomes a lovely broad grassy track, which crosses a byway, and becomes extremely wide when it meets the minor road leading to Hindon (suitable for parking). A brief left turn down this road and then right between the hedges. (Here if you wish to save time and do more roadwork you may divert south of Hindon, to Berwick St Leonard and up to A303.) This brings you out onto the B3089 which you cross. Straight on past the tumulus and to the next minor road, where you turn left (902338) and then right

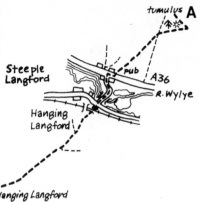

down next bridlepath, a grassy track between hedges, rather overgrown. At the next minor road turn left into Chicklade. You meet here the A303, a nasty busy road, so take care.

Straight over onto another metal road, which turns into a track leading up Cratt Hill. Over (slightly to the right) at the track you meet (904360) and at fork, turn right.

This track follows Great Ridge and the Roman road, and is a delightful ride, with rolling country all round. Coming down through the woods towards the A303, you keep to the north of the woods by the road, and turn right to cross the main road (take care), going straight on to another track. Diversion B if going to Mr Puddy (see notes at end of route). At the crossroads of tracks turn left (964343) and continue over open country until you cross over two minor roads close together; keep straight on until (007348) the paths fork, when you go to the left and over the minor road to Dinton. This track turns into a

bridlepath and carries on to Hanging Langford, where you turn right down the minor road and then left, over the river (if it's hot, this is a popular bathing place) to Steeple Langford. Here you have a short stretch on the busy A36 before turning left up a metal road track leading north-east.

At the crossroads go straight over and on to the next crossroads (054384) where you turn left (tumulus on left). Straight on till you again meet the A303 (dual carriageway at this point), straight over to the Yarnbury Castle earthwork which you leave on your left. The three banks and ditches enclose an area of 28 acres.

Where the tracks meet, take the mid turn in front of you (or alternatively turn right and follow track going north-easterly; but this means going up the A360, a busy road, into Tilshead). Cross several

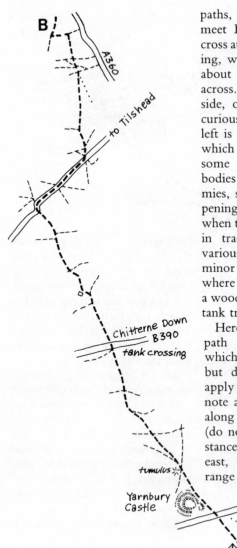

paths, but continue north till you meet B390 (021435) which you cross at what is called a tank crossing, with bollards; do not worry about the bollards, go straight across. Beautiful rolling countryside, only marred by tanks and curious military exercises. To the left is Ministry of Defence land, which is safe, but may result in some odd occurrences, such as bodies advancing on their tummies, smoke and so on. All happenings less likely in August, when they go on holiday. At fork in tracks, turn left and cross various other tracks till reaching minor road leading to Tilshead where you turn right till you meet a wood on the right and a maze of tank tracks on the left.

Here you may use a permissive path provided by the MoD, which avoids going up the A360, but does mean that you must apply for permission to do so (see note at end of route). You skirt along the edge of the danger area (do not enter under any circumstances); take track leading northeast, and make sure you keep range danger signs always on your

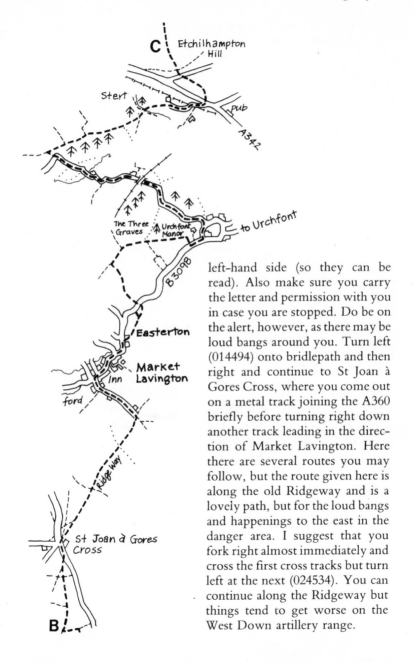

left-hand side (so they can be read). Also make sure you carry the letter and permission with you in case you are stopped. Do be on the alert, however, as there may be loud bangs around you. Turn left (014494) onto bridlepath and then right and continue to St Joan à Gores Cross, where you come out on a metal track joining the A360 briefly before turning right down another track leading in the direction of Market Lavington. Here there are several routes you may follow, but the route given here is along the old Ridgeway and is a lovely path, but for the loud bangs and happenings to the east in the danger area. I suggest that you fork right almost immediately and cross the first cross tracks but turn left at the next (024534). You can continue along the Ridgeway but things tend to get worse on the West Down artillery range.

Meet the minor road and go into Market Lavington. You will pass a ford on the left where you could water your horse. At the B3098 turn right and continue to Easterton, and onto OS173.

This road is not too bad, and you soon turn off left up the track marked 'Easterton Sands', going right at the next road, then left and up the track to the right towards the Three Graves. If going to Mrs Firth (see notes) you will turn right again but otherwise go on towards Urchfont, where the track turns sharp right to bring you out again on the B3098. (Here, if doing Alternative A, you cross the road. The advantage of Alternative A is that you go up Tan Hill to the Wansdyke and through some lovely countryside. The disadvantage is that you have a long stretch of minor road through All Cannings.) The main route now takes you left after the manor up the minor road (037568) Urchfont to Potterne. You must stick to this road (it's not busy, quite delightful) until the sign for 'Potterne' and the road bends to the left. Here you go straight ahead up the bridlepath and at the T junction of tracks turn right. Follow the bridlepath turning sharp right where another track comes in ahead.

Through Stert and onto minor road which crosses the A342. Follow track ahead leading north-

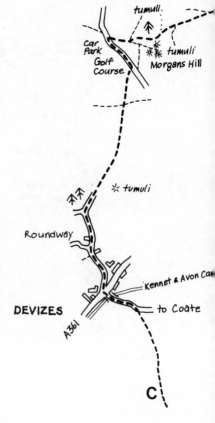

westerly over minor and straight on bridlepath over Etchilhampton Hill and on to meet the minor road to Coate, where turning left brings you into Devizes and onto the A361. Beware traffic here; you must turn left for a few yards and then take road through industrial estate to the right. Through Roundway (forking right) on to next fork (014639) where turn right and follow hard road, with broad grassy verges (good place for parking) till it turns into a grassy track. Cross another track till veering to the right and meeting the minor road. Turn left briefly along the road, then follow the diverted bridlepath which follows the road on the left, between the golf course and the road, to the right of the old thorn hedge, marking the old course of the bridlepath. Cross the road and straight onto another marked track which leads you along the old Roman Road (forking left) and up Morgans Hill.

At crossroad of paths (048680), fork left again, which leads towards Oldbury Castle and the White Horse. Fork right, passing north of the gallops on a permissive path (ignore sign saying 'Racehorses') and arrive on the A4. A short stretch on this busy road will bring you to a drive on left and also the bridlepath, approached through a parking area. A good stretch of turf is ahead and, bearing left, you arrive just to the right of a barn, on the minor road (089698). Turn right and follow track which turns into a small metal path, wending through water meadows, going left over a small bridge and bringing you out beside Avebury Manor. Turn right in front of a row of cottages, and you find the main street, leading left. This will take you through the stone circle at Avebury and, crossing the A361, onto another metal route, which takes you up to Overton Down. Here you turn left on to the Countryside Commission Ridgeway path, which is well marked with signposts for its whole length.

DLF 55

To: The Range Safety Officer

_____

_____

APPLICATION FOR PERMISSION TO ENTER THE

                    IMBER   **RANGES**

Name of Applicant _____.

Address _____

Age _____   Occupation _____

1. I apply for permission to enter the ____IMBER_____ Ranges as under:-

    (a) Date _____ (b) Time _____

    (c) Place to be visited ___AREA 10 A_____

    (d) Route TILSHEAD TO GORE x FARM — AS SHOWN ON MAP

    (e) Method of Transport (motor vehicle, pedal cycle, on foot etc)

        HORSE

2. Purpose of entry:- ___TO BY-PASS THE A 360_____

3. I have read and understand the Notes, Conditions and Warnings attached to this Application and I agree to the Conditions. I am aware that there are hazards and dangerous things on the Ranges and I enter AT MY OWN RISK. In particular, I understand that if I enter the Ranges I may be injured, incapacitated or killed and that my property may be damaged or destroyed as a result of those hazards or by those dangerous things. I VOLUNTARILY ACCEPT THE RISKS INVOLVED.

4. I agree with the Secretary of State for Defence that if permission is granted to enter the Ranges neither I nor my personal representatives nor my dependants shall have or make any claim for injury (including injury resulting in death) or damage against the Crown or the Secretary of State or any officer, agent, servant, workman or contractor of the Crown in respect of the state or condition of the land for the time being, or any dangerous thing on or below or above the ground there.

5. I further agree to indemnify the Crown against all payments made by the Crown to its servants or agents (whether or not they are paid in pursuance of a legally enforceable obligation) for the purpose of indemnifying them against any such claim as aforesaid.

Date _____

Signature of Applicant _____

Witness:

    Signature _____

    Address _____

    _____

    Occupation _____

/HTc

Notes

1. Permission from MoD to use permissive path near Tisbury is obtained from
    PSA
    Defence Land Agent
    Durrington
    Salisbury SP4 8AF
    tel: 0980 52629

Alternative A

Is closer to the original Ridgeway but involves more roadwork. It also leads along the Wansdyke (a post-Roman road which ran from near Inkpen to the Bristol Channel) and Tan Hill, which are lovely stretches of Downs. Divert from main route at the B3098 at Urchfont, where you turn right off B3098 instead of left, continue to A342, where you follow the road to the right briefly, then turn left to Chirton down metal road. Continue down this road crossing Kennet and Avon Canal until you meet the minor road to Stanton St Bernard, where you turn left and almost immediately down bridleway. Or you can carry straight on when you meet the road. The various routes go over All Cannings Down, Thorn Hill and East Kennet.

Alternative B

To take in Mr Puddy's riding school if you are staying there, divert from main route at A303 where instead of going south over Chilmark Down you turn north through Stockton Wood and then Sherrington, Codford St Mary and over Clay Pit Hill to meet up with main route at Chitterne Down (021434).

Possible accommodation

Mr W. D. Puddy, White Horse Trekking Centre, Codford, Warminster, Wiltshire. Tel. (0985) 50395. Horses only. Various inns nearby for riders.

Mrs Malcolm Firth, Eastcott Manor, Devizes, Wiltshire. Tel. (038 081) 3313. Stabling and sometimes grazing.

4 Avebury to Stonehenge

Sam Hart

Approx. 53½k, 33½ miles

OS maps 173, 184

Start: 100700:OS 173

Finish: 122422:OS 184

Avebury and Stonehenge are two of the most popular pre-historic sites in Wiltshire. As the crow flies, they are only 15 miles apart, but this route follows the best bridleways and takes the rider to Oldbury Castle above the Cherhill White Horse, along 6 miles of the

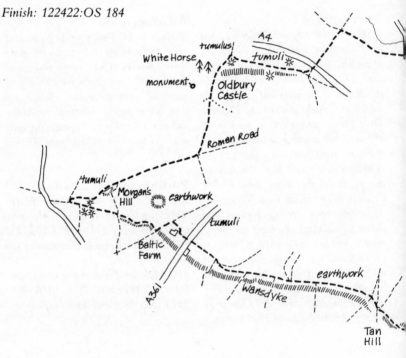

Wansdyke from Morgans Hill (028672) to Knap Hill (120635). It then descends to cross the Pewsey Vale (3 miles of roadwork) to climb up onto the eastern end of Salisbury Plain. The rider is now on MoD land and the existing bridleways are plentiful, but a

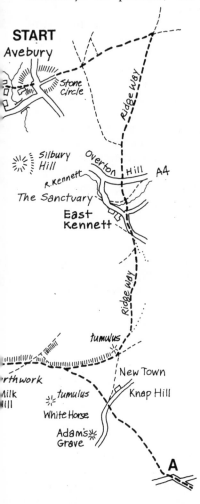

compass is needed to keep to the correct one. The route crosses the Avon at Ablington (158468) before crossing more plain for Larkhill and Stonehenge. Total distance of 33½ miles, with only about 6 miles of roadwork.

Leave Avebury in westerly direction, proceeding down the main street from the Red Lion and crossing the River Kennet which near its source is a mere stream. In 1 mile, a signpost directs you to Windmill Hill to the north, but carry on westerly for another mile to next track intersection at clump of beech trees. Take south-west track leading to A4 and another bigger clump of beeches.

Once across the A4 hard roads are behind you and you can look forward to 10 miles of downland tracks with beautiful going and lovely views. Climb a rise for about 200 yards and then turn west, following an ancient linear earthwork. The temptation will be to have a canter on the open downland to the south with downland views and Beckhampton gallops in the valley, but the rider will need to stick to the earthworks, even negotiating an iron gate with a stile beside it. Follow the earthworks for about a mile before turning south and up a chalky path that leads to a tin barn. Here another iron gate with a stile beside it opens for the track to take you, still uphill, to yet a third gate, where a notice signifies you are now entering a Nature Conservancy Area, enclosing Oldbury Castle.

If you divert from the track to explore Oldbury Castle and the huge pencil-like monument in its centre (built by the Marquis of Lansdowne in 1845 to commemorate his great ancestor, Sir William Petty, founder of the family fortunes), or ride over to stand above the ear of the Cherhill White Horse on the northern escarpment; remember your exit gate is in the south-east corner of the enclosure and again marked with a Nature Conservancy board. The Cherhill White Horse was the work of Dr Alsop of Calne in 1780. On leaving Oldbury, if you dismount to negotiate the gate, you will see on the horizon to your south-west, two wireless masts which mark the summit of Morgans Hill, your next destination.

Descend southward from Oldbury Castle; flints, arrowheads, Roman pottery and coins have all been found in the twenty acres of Oldbury ramparts, but I thought the 17th-century pocket sundial was most interesting, with its inscription:

Set me right and use me well
And I the time to you will tell

Carry on till you reach a belt of trees, turn westward along a lovely grassy track which is part of a Roman Road, till you reach Morgans Hill. On the west side of the hill you turn 45° from travelling westerly to south-easterly. In fact you now follow the Wansdyke, which is thought to have been built between 300 and 800 AD. There is no conclusive evidence on its purpose. It stretches east to west from Savernake Forest towards the Bristol Channel and has disappeared in places. But on the northern escarpment of the Marlborough Downs which guard the Vale of Pewsey the ditches are as deep as those at Maiden Castle or Old Sarum. They seem to guard against an enemy from the north. The Saxons advancing up the Thames and Kennet valleys? The frontier of King Alfred's Wessex? Or a later boundary between Saxon tribes? No one knows for certain but it is certainly very impressive as you ride along its crest.

The Wansdyke is quite a shallow ditch at first and before you get to Shepherd's Shore on the A361 you need to divert to pass through Baltic Farm and rejoin the Wansdyke a mile further on. At Shepherd's Shore a cottage and farm buildings on each side of the road completely block the bridle-path. From now on simply follow the Wansdyke. On top of the hills it is now some 20 to 30 feet deep and sometimes you'll need to ride on one side and sometimes on the other; sometimes at the bottom of the ditch. When you meet a hard

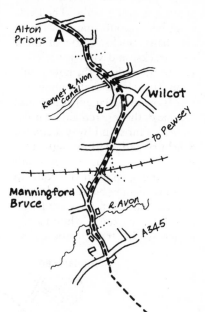

New Town Farm and across a minor road, through several gateways. If you miss this south-east turn, you can backtrack in half a mile south along the southern projection of the Ridgeway, or even follow the same Ridgeway north and return to Avebury, making a round trip of 18 miles (a pleasant day's ride).

However, once across the road at Knap Hill the track takes you south-east to the minor road from Alton Priors to Pewsey (a delightful old track with hedges, leading downhill). You have three or four miles of roadwork on minor roads, because there are no bridleways across the Vale of Pewsey. Follow the signposts to Wilcot where you cross the Kennet and Avon canal and then at Wilcot follow the

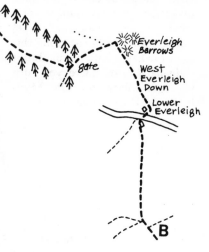

surfaced road (100648) do not be tempted to follow the road in either direction (south leads you to a Nature Reserve) but instead go through one of those fence gates that are hard to discern and continue along the Wansdyke (where you will find some overgrown jumps running alongside it). When it swings north-east you need to leave it and travel south-east across some downland till, on topping the rise, you can pick up your bearings to pass south of signpost to Manningford and then Manningford Bruce, where you cross the upper reaches of the Avon. Then at last across the A345 onto another bridleway which takes you up onto Bruce Down. You will have to watch the electric fences here, and keep to the north of the beech belt to find that the iron exit gate onto WD land is midway in the fence between the two beech belts and not as shown on map – be warned.

Once on WD land, recognizable because of its absence of wire fences and hedges, turn north-east to a group of barrows, where you pick up a track leading south-east to Lower Everleigh and onto map 184, Salisbury Plain.

At Lower Everleigh, cross the A342 and proceed through the farm, but at the end of the track make sure you go south down a valley to the minor road in 1½ miles. Turn north-east along this road for half a mile to an abrupt right-hand turn. Here you turn south to follow the Old Marlborough Road. This is an old coach road, now grassed over, unless cut up by tanks. The landscape here is confusing, since there are many tracks, some of them tank tracks, and your route takes you to the right of the new plantation. In 1½ miles (heading towards the firing range) you should see one of the few remaining milestones, almost midway between Salisbury and Marlborough. Unfortunately as you travel south across the open plain you come to the outer danger boards of the rifle ranges, and if red flags are flying from hilltops and a white barrier is across the track, proceed no

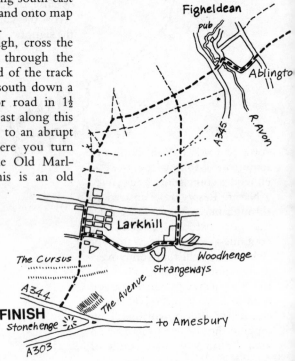

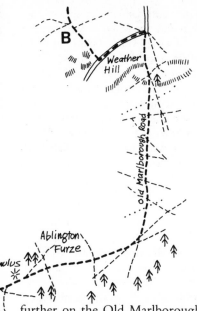

many fir plantations across Nine Mile River (a Winterbourne stream) near Sheep Bridge. Take the metal road through Bulford Barracks and across the A303 to pass west of Amesbury, past Salisbury Clumps to cross the A345 down a track to Great Durnford across the Avon and approach Stonehenge from the south via Springbottom Farm.

However, if you have come through Figheldean, you must try to get the correct route through Larkhill (as long as no red flags are flying). Travel south-west and then on topping brow of the hill you will see Larkhill Race Course and further south half a dozen water tanks. The water tanks are surrounded by belts of trees; you need to find your way to the western end of them to find the main road south through the barracks (don't be tempted to take the most westerly road out or you will find your exit blocked). Over the B3086 and through more barracks. Lots of open grass spaces around all the buildings, but unfortunately 'keep off the grass' and not until you are clear of the married quarters do you leave the macadam road for a trackway leading to Stonehenge.

If the red flags are flying, then turn south before this and down track (144462) through barrier over minor road to Strangways past Woodhenge and then turn west to join bridleway.

further on the Old Marlborough Rd, but turn westerly to climb the ridge between Ablington Furze and the Wig, where a high water tank is your landmark, before descending down a track to Ablington, a hamlet south of Figheldean.

Ablington must have some of the loveliest cottages in Wiltshire, and all well restored by the Ministry of Defence and a delight to ride through. Here you take a sharp right-angle turn by Figheldean School to cross the Avon and the A345 to proceed southwest up a track onto the plain again. Again, the number of tracks is confusing. If no red flags are flying on the Old Marlborough Rd, then continue through the

5 Cerne Abbas Giant to Stonehenge

Sam Hart

Approx. 79k, 50 miles

OS maps 194, 195, 184

Start: 670013:OS 194

Finish: 122422:OS 184

This route can be used in conjunction with the Ridgeway to connect the Cerne Abbas Giant with the Uffington White Horse. (See Ridgeway route, p. 13.) Although the total length of this would only be 65 miles, it is many more following the trackways and bridleways from the hills of Dorset, Cranborne Chase, Salisbury Plain, across the Marlborough Downs and to the Berkshire Downs. Surely a connoisseur's route, visiting Stonehenge and Avebury, as you cross the heart of Wessex. (On approaching Avebury, the diversion to Morgans Hill can be avoided if desired. From Stonehenge follow this route, then from the Wansdyke a bridlepath takes you up to the roundabout at Beckhampton on the A4.)

From Cerne Abbas on OS 194 a bridleway leads you easterly steeply through the gorse up the side of the Giant to the Giant's Head camping site and, after a

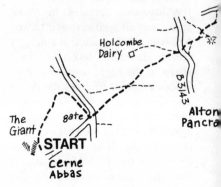

gate at the side of the road, proceeds south down the road which runs north south-east and above Cerne Abbas. Turn easterly off this road and continue downwards for three-quarters of a mile until reaching the B3143 where the track is joined by that leading to Holcombe Dairy. Once across the B3143 the bridleway travels eastwards to join a farm track from Ball Hill and the woods. (If travelling in the opposite direction, be careful, the bridleway can easily be missed where it diverts westward.) Several bridleways run parallel to each other here, but I prefer the northern of the two which keeps to the high ground north of Church Hill. Cross the minor road at Armswell Farm and continue to the Dorsetshire Gap where the bridleways converge. A

turn east takes you to the edge of Hill Wood, and, continuing north by Breach Wood, you turn right, avoiding Melcombe Park, a huge wood.

Cross a minor road 100 yards south of Hatherly Farm and traverse along 20 yards of the bed of a stream, with gates across the stream at both ends. Quite an obstacle if your horse dislikes water and won't stand still whilst you open gates. Then proceed through several fields and gates till after 1½ miles you come to the ancient earthworks at Rawlsbury, and Bulbarrow Hill picnic spot

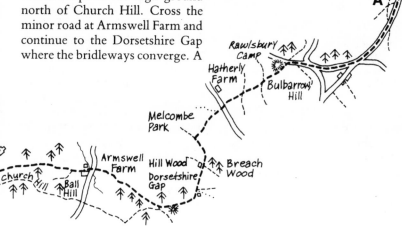

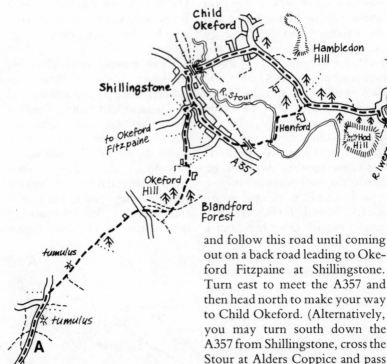

with its huge radio masts. The map shows the bridleway passing along the south-east edge of the earthworks, but you head for the cross in the middle of the rings. Here, at the iron wicker gate, you join the road going east for ½ mile before branching off north-east towards the back road from Okeford Fitzpaine to Winterbourne Stickland, which you cross. From Okeford Hill you descend steeply to join a very minor road appearing at the edge of Blandford Forest

and follow this road until coming out on a back road leading to Okeford Fitzpaine at Shillingstone. Turn east to meet the A357 and then head north to make your way to Child Okeford. (Alternatively, you may turn south down the A357 from Shillingstone, cross the Stour at Alders Coppice and pass through Hanford to meet up with this route past Child Okeford. This route necessitates negotiating five field gates and needs accurate map-reading.) Turn east to Child Okeford and turn south down the A350 for a short distance, passing in the dip between Hambledon Hill and Hod Hill. Then take the bridleway known as Smuggler's Lane going east in the Stour and Iwerne Valley. Then on to map OS 195.

You emerge on the north-south minor road from Shaftesbury to

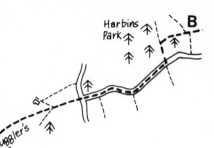

Blandford, known as the Royal Road, which you cross and continue on back roads eastward towards Tarrant Gunville. Before reaching Tarrant Gunville turn north to Harbin's Park and then east to Stubhampton, a straggling village which runs into Tarrant Gunville. The bridleway is not signposted at this road, but you come out close to the water-pumping house at the side of the road. Here two routes are now open to you: either east to Ashmore Bottom and Well Bottom and round the pond to Ashmore or north to Stubhampton Bottom and Washers Pit. Old Dorset legends claim that until the bones in an old barrow near Washers Pit were removed to Ashmore churchyard, when the road to Fontmell was built, one could hear the wailing of the wild spirits of the woods, called Gabbygammies. But a hunting horn is said to signal the escape of a lady who was hanging by her hair from an ash tree over the well at Washers Pit.

You are now in the middle of Cranborne Chase, which lies to the south of you. Nearly 3 times larger than the New Forest, Cranborne Chase is now totally enclosed and farmed, whereas the New Forest still boasts extensive open spaces and wasteland. This was no doubt due to the soil fertility which encouraged landowners to encroach and eventually enslave the Chase. It was established by the early Norman kings, but gradually passed through various offspring and royal lords to the Cecils, who became Earls of Salisbury; but the Pembrokes of Wilton House and the Shaftesburys also had their interests. In more recent years the Pitt family and the Rivers were 'lords of the chase' and their successor General Pitt-Rivers became well known for his archaeological activities. He was the last of the lords of the chase with the right to hunt deer wherever they were found and with the obligation on the other hand to preserve 'vert and venison'; he received from Parliament an annual payment for the annulment of his rights and privileges on other people's land.

Enclosed the Chase may be, but with its network of bridleways and its combes and rolling downs on the chalk, its woods and copses on the clay and greensands, it makes you want to stop and explore rather than merely pass through. But pass through you must if you wish to reach your journey's end.

Either way you end up at

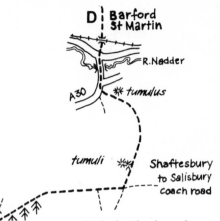

long spurs which divide the valleys of the Wylye, Nadder and Ebble (all of which wind down to Salisbury) and to cross those valleys before reaching Stonehenge.

Keep to the high ground and you come down onto the Ox Drove (if going in the opposite direction, be careful when you leave the Ox Drove and follow the hard road not to go down the hill, but keep high). Follow the Ox Drove to come to a track going north to Alvediston where you arrive beside a pub. Now you are getting into the Ebble Valley, a lovely valley with its villages of Broad Chalke, Bowerchalke and Ebbesborne Wake. We cannot linger but must go on to West End where a track will lead you northeast (ignore fork to the west) to the old Shaftesbury–Salisbury coach road (another green track). This old green road goes north-

Ashmore with its famous pond, ¾ acre in size and 15 feet deep, 700 feet above sea level, on a chalk down, and last dried out in 1911, right in the middle of the village. Your road leads north onto the B3081 and the Wiltshire/Dorset border, where you should stop and look east and west to rolling downs and deep combes; stand and wonder.

Take the minor road north and branch off to the east to Win Green, which is owned by the National Trust and at 277 metres is the highest point in south Wiltshire. Well worth stopping to look north again. You are about to use two old green roads, to cross the

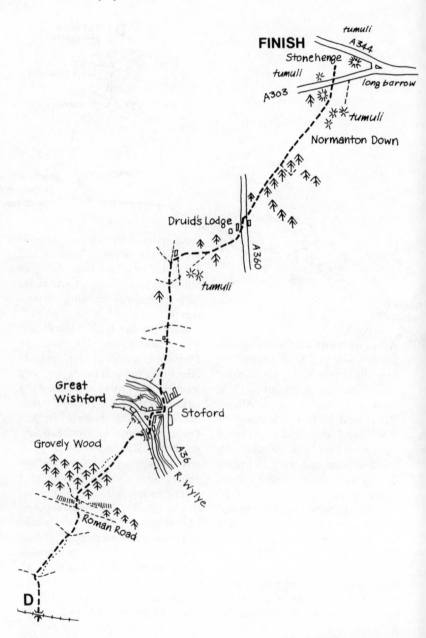

FINISH

tumuli

A344

Stonehenge

tumuli

A303

long barrow

tumuli

Normanton Down

Druid's Lodge

A360

tumuli

Great
Wishford

Stoford

Grovely Wood

A36

R. Wylye

Roman Road

D

east, passing Fovant Hut and above the army badges carved on the side of Fovant Down, past Chiselbury Camp. In just over a mile you must swing north on a plateau and follow a track winding north and west towards Barford St Martin. You come out on the A30, and after $\frac{1}{4}$ mile of the busy road cross the River Nadder and continue to the Green Dragon. A hard road now takes you north to the bridleway which was the old Shaftesbury–Salisbury coach road which skirts Grovely Wood on the south side. Look down now onto the valley of the Nadder.

Continue north-east and climb into Grovely Wood, 4 miles of beautiful woodland, 4 miles long but only 1 to 2 miles wide, and on its long axis a broad avenue of copper beech lies along the route of the Roman Road from Old Sarum to the Mendips. Cross this avenue, which is at its best in spring, when a carpet of bluebells underlies the copper beeches. A hard chalky track descends to Wishford, going under a railway bridge and meeting the back road to Wilton. Unless you wish to eat at the Royal Oak in Wishford, go

north to the church, briefly join the A36 and soon turn off this on a track heading north. Pause to study a century of bread prices carved on the corner wall of the churchyard and if it is Oakapple Day you may meet the villagers of Great Wishford returning from Grovely Wood with token branches en route to Salisbury Cathedral to assert for ever their immemorial right to gather firewood in the forest behind them: a right wrested years ago from the ancestors of the Earl of Pembroke.

Over the water meadows and up a wide grassy track leading up to the downs where you can look down on beautiful views of the Wylye Valley with a background of Grovely Wood. This track brings you out on to a hard road where you turn east towards Druid's Lodge and the A360, which you join briefly and cross onto a track to Normanton Down. This brings you out at the A303, which you cross to follow a bridleway going west of Stonehenge before crossing the A344 and resuming the route to Uffington.

6 Wilton to Hindon and return

Sam Hart

Approx. 46k, 28¾ miles

OS map 184

Start: 090318:OS 184

This route starts on the western side of Wilton, which is not only the ancient capital of Wessex, but the home of the Pembroke family, who acquired it by gift from Henry VIII at the dissolution of the monasteries. The route follows the Roman Road from Old Sarum to the Mendips via Grovely Wood and the Great Ridge woods to Hindon and back following the old coach road Salisbury to Exeter. Leave Wilton by the A30, but where the A30 turns sharply west take the back road to Ditchampton under the railway bridge. Immediately turn west up past Wilton Middle School and climb north-west up the track to Grovely Wood.

In half a mile, by an old tin barn, the track forks. The westerly fork is the Salisbury–Exeter coach road

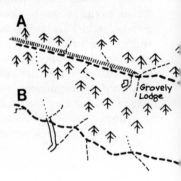

(your return route) so keep to the easterly track and again at another fork in about 50 yards. On entering Grovely Wood, you have 1½ miles of a straight wide avenue, with a hard track down the middle, but ample trotting or cantering space each side. Not that you will want to hurry if it is spring. The copper beeches and the carpet of bluebells are beyond description.

At this end of this wide avenue, the bridleway goes straight on past some pheasant pens to Grovely Lodge and is often overgrown; a slight diversion keeps to the hard track which still leads you to the north side of Grovely Lodge. Here the track follows the Roman Road westward and straight for another two miles; here the old beech and deciduous trees have been in places replanted by conifers.

Once clear of Grovely Wood you cross the Wylye to Dinton back road at the top of the hill, and have to link south and west round a copse to pick up the Salisbury–Exeter coach road. Disappointingly this has been concreted by a local farmer for a way, but you soon come to a green road, inviting a canter. It is impossible to pick up the Roman Road again till you reach Great Ridge. When you reach the back road from the A303 to Teffont Magna turn north towards the A303, but on reaching the fork down to Chilmark, cross over and take the brideway to the A303 past Down Farm and so across the A303 to Stockton Wood.

Locals can find their way dodging around Stockton Wood to get to the Great Ridge but strangers had better head north-west across the earthworks, until you can look down on the lovely country between Great Ridge and the Wylye Valley, my favourite part of Wiltshire.

A sharp descent still proceeding north-west brings you to a hard road where you turn abruptly south-west to climb to the Great Ridge, even though other tracks and bridleways might tempt you away to explore. Back up on the Great Ridge you turn west along a straight broad avenue a mile long. This avenue must be 40 yards wide, and grass from side to side.

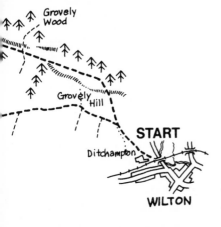

It invites you to a scamper, but if you proceed quietly, you may well sight deer or foxes crossing over. At the end is a track, and again this is only halfway through Great Ridge and the bridleway ahead may be overgrown so be prepared to link north, before regaining your original route west. Another mile to the end of the woods and again a straight track, which, if you travel in spring, is ablaze with rhododendrons.

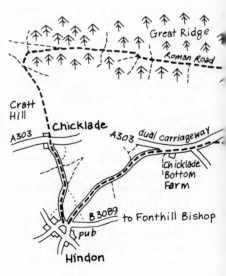

Once clear of Great Ridge, you turn south round the edge of the wood and descend by a track to recross the A303 at Chicklade and so up the hill to Hindon.

The Lamb Inn at Hindon was once an important coaching inn and Hindon itself of considerable importance. Since the pike trusts built the A303 a mile or two north of Hindon and the old green coach roads were abandoned, Hindon has tended to ossify. However, it is still a very attractive village and a good meal can be had at the Lamb Inn which is a very hospitable place.

Although the old coach road can be traced west of Hindon where it crosses the A303 and across the Downs north of Mere, before descending Whitesheet Hill I think the best section is eastward back to Wilton.

Leave Hindon on the B3089 for Fonthill Bishop, but at the edge of the village (Hindon) turn north on a road that leads you to the A303 at Chicklade Bottom Farm.

Do not cross the dual carriageway here but keep on the wide verge for 50 yards till you come to the back road down to Fonthill Bishop. The old coach road was diverted here when they built the dual carriageway but a little research will find a track parallel and 20 yards from the A303 leading to a gate into a field and of course leading eastward.

Inside the gate follow the line of

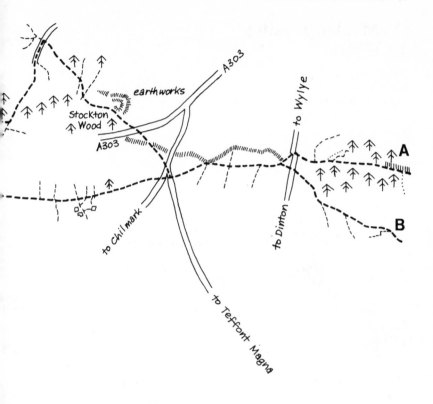

the hedge (no track) to the top. Where the hedge turns south, head due east across a big field, until you find a gate and a track between hedges, still heading east. Now you can start looking for old milestones, often hidden in the long grass. Follow this track through several gates until you reach the A303 Chilmark back road.

You will now recognize the next stretch from your outward journey but when you reach the Wylye – Dinton back road, you pass to the south of a small copse, which you passed on its north side on your outward journey. The green coach road avoided Grovely Wood and skirted along the rolling downs south of the woods, downs which were in coaching days open country. Even now a broad green track takes you the 4½ miles back to Wilton, with no navigation headaches and having seen the best of Wiltshire.

7 Maiden Bradley to Wilton

Pat Kingston

Approx. 50k, 31 miles

OS maps 183, 184

Start: 802390:OS 183
Finish: 090318:OS 184

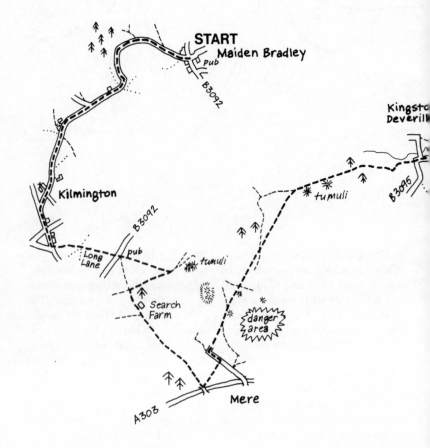

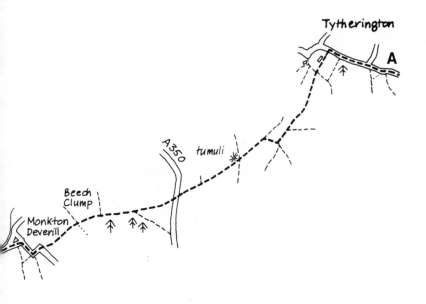

Start at Maiden Bradley (where there is a pub) and take back roads west to Kilmington, turning east off the back road down Long Lane and then heading south to Mere. From Mere turn north-east and follow bridleway past Danger Area over lovely country and through Kingston Deverill, briefly on the B3095 and then at Monkton Deverill again taking the bridleway past tumulus and clumps of beech trees to go straight over the A350 and onto map OS 184 (890383). Still on the bridleway continue to Tytherington and Corton on the metal road. From Corton take rupps and bridleways to Boyton Down and over the A303 to Teffont Down and then onto the tracks that lead to Grovely Wood (see previous route Wilton to Hindon).

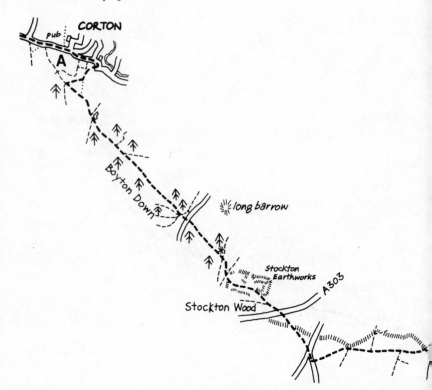

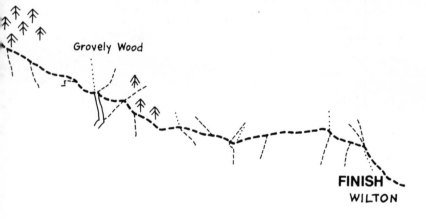

8 The South Downs Way

Sheila Beardall

Approx. 120k, 75 miles

OS maps 197, 198, 199

Start: 722182:OS 197

Finish: 596981: OS 199

Although Queen Elizabeth Forest is not for some people the beginning of the South Downs Way, it is a good place to start since it has a car park. The car parks are by the A3 and there is also a forest information centre with café, and horsebox car park with hitching rails. Follow the tracks uphill to get to the centre and then take the lane and go through Sunwood Farm; on crossing the boundary to Hampshire, you join what is the accepted South Downs Way.

Into Forty Acre Lane, cross the B2146, then the B2141 and follow alongside it for a spell before crossing it again and going to-

wards Harting Downs, where there is a car park and picnic area. Wonderful grassy slopes lead you away from Harting and on to Beacon Hill. The track takes you to a narrow lane, though you can ride to the summit of Beacon Hill. The way descends into a hollow and wends its way up Pen Hill and then down to a sharp left and right by Buriton Farm (820179).

You then ascend to Philliswood Down and through a wood on the slopes of Treyford Hill before taking a lane leading over Didling Hill and continuing south of the summit of Linch Down (813 feet). The path now takes you to Cock-

ing Down and is bordered in parts by woodland; occasionally these give way to wonderful views across Hampshire. The stretch before you reach the A286 is one of the most enjoyable of all the South Downs Way; it feels isolated, although the map tells of hamlets nestling in the lee of the downs if riders felt like braving the steep descent down. A flinty track takes you to the road just south of Cocking and rises up to enter forests along the tops of the downs. Bridleways lead off on both sides of the downs going through the woods to Graffham, Singleton and West Dean – all traditional Sussex

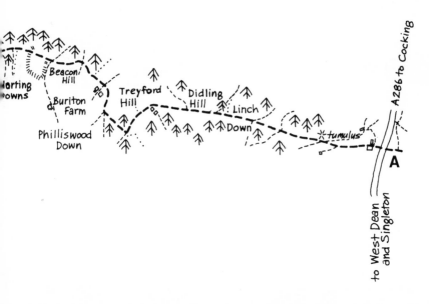

villages. The way leads straight for many miles (although there is a diversion possible to the north, and out of the woods). The track is completely enclosed by woods until you reach a pleasant stretch of good going above Graffham; then again the way becomes heavily shrouded with woods and there is little to see from the top.

You climb up to Littleton Down, which at 837 feet is the highest point on the downs and take a steep path down across two fields and on to Littleton Farm where you cross the A285. Again the way rises, twisting and turning as a stony track up to the summit of Bignor Hill, where it crosses Stane Street, an old Roman Road (970129). You are now at 737 feet and may well find a lot of visitors to this National Trust area. The narrow grassy track descends,

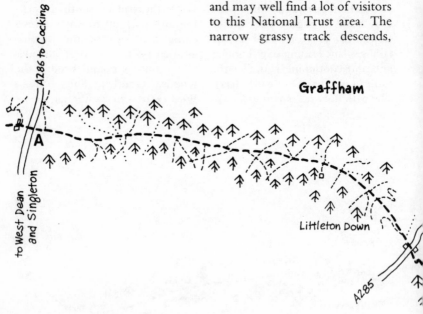

keeping Houghton Forest on its right and dropping down to the A29.

From now on, the character of the downs changes from being heavily wooded and with views rare from the summits to being much more open downland. Cross the main A29 and over a couple of arable fields before taking a right-hand turn into a lane where another right-hand turn will take you to a long stone bridge over the River Arun and on past Amberley station. You must follow the B2139 for a further short stretch before turning right down a quiet lane past deep chalk pits on either side.

A very steep slippery slope leads you to Amberley Mount and then gently descends by a wider track to a car park and carries on along-side more fields. Another car park at Chantry Port at Storrington and then through several cattle grids to a wonderful section of the way, with views across rolling hills to the sea and over the Weald to-wards the North Downs. Here are attractive bridleways to explore to the south, although sunny week-ends bring walkers and picnickers out in force. Onto map 198.

Rise again to the summit of Highden Hill, where the route is a stony track and leads down past a rubbish tip and into a steep lane. A detour, more pleasant for riders and horses, takes you left up a track to Washington on an easier route over a special riders' and walkers' bridge just past Rowdell House over the A24. Go through Washington and right to rejoin the way. The way proper is a very badly eroded chalk track which crosses the A24 south of Wash-ington. Numerous other bridle-ways tempt one to explore them in this area.

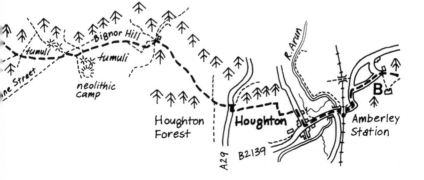

Storrington

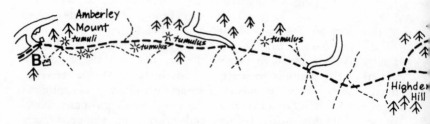

Grassy stretches lead you south of Chanctonbury Hill and over Steyning Round Hill where the tracks become rather hard, but avoid the village of Steyning. Turn right along the Sompting to Steyning lane but turn left off this to follow the way alongside a couple of arable fields and then on a good, fast track leading to a couple of gates and onto a track that brings you out onto a metal road. Turn right down this lovely country lane to pass Annington Manor and Annington Farm before crossing the Adur on a new bridge and taking a quick zig-zag across the A283. Lancing College is to your right and the track rises, passing the youth hostel and Trueleigh Hill Farm. Bypassing Edburton Hill and passing over Perching Hill, you are able to enjoy one of the loveliest stretches. The way runs parallel with the lane to Devil's Dyke where there is a modern hotel with restaurant and self-service

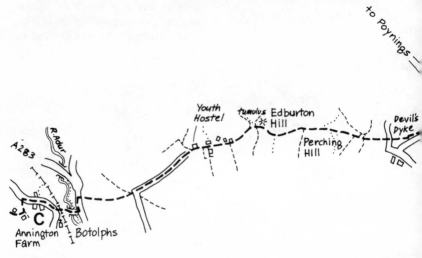

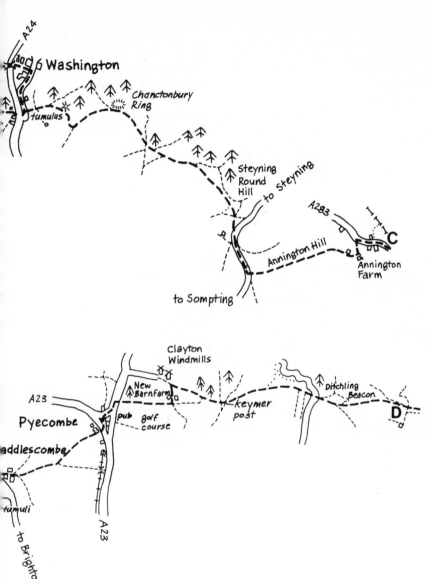

A24

to Washington

Chanctonbury
Ring

tumulus

Steyning
Round
Hill

to Steyning

A283

C

Annington Hill

Annington
Farm

to Sompting

Clayton
Windmills

New
Barnfarm

A23

Keymer
post

Ditchling
Beacon

D

Pyecombe

pub   golf
course

addlescombe

tumuli

to Brighton

A23

cafeteria. The deep combes are a popular venue for hang gliders and other visitors. Now the route drops steeply past a reservoir and crosses the Brighton to Poynings road. From the lovely little village of Saddlescombe, where only the farm machinery seems to have moved with the times, the way climbs as a narrow lane to West Hill, past Brendon riding centre and through the back roads of Pyecombe village.

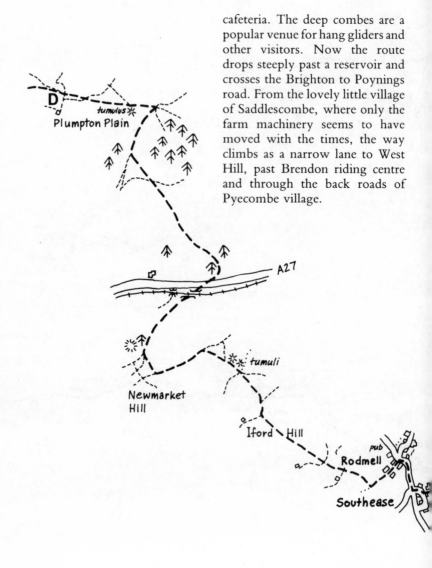

Having crossed the busy A23 the way follows beside a golf course and then runs sharply north through New Barn Farm and then right past Clayton windmills – better known as Jack and Jill – and up again towards Ditchling Beacon. Keymer Post marks the boundary between East and West Sussex and the way passes two dewponds before reaching the popular tourist spot of the Beacon (813 feet). From here the way meanders along the top of the downs, takes a turn towards Lewes at a junction of bridleways, passes the end of a mixed wood and leads through a sheep pound. High up on Plumpton Plain, the route covers some lovely tracks before descending to cross the main A27 dual carriageway by Newmarket Inn.

The track now rises and takes a right-hand turn to climb over Newmarket Hill and Iford Hill, where there is a right and then a left turn. Passing through several gates, you drop down via Mill Lane into Rodmell. You must turn right for Southease at the busy road in Rodmell, cross the River Ouse and the railway (there is a telephone and self-service barrier) and finally the busy Newhaven road. The twisting uphill route now leads to Firle Beacon, with superb views all around. This is one of the highest points (713 feet) and attracts many visitors on sunny weekends, and also a smattering of gliders. Grassy stretches

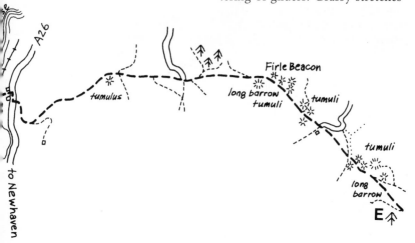

lead away from Firle Beacon (and onto OS 199) but turn into a rather monotonous track to Alfriston, where riders are directed through the picturesque market square and over two bridges. Here again the temptation is to linger. The way rises to Windover Hill, before turning into Church Lane at Jevington.

Although there are no shops, there is a pub and a restaurant. Turning right and then left, you find yourself in a deep lane rising up to two tracks, one (the lower) beautifully grassy, whilst the higher is more stony. A major crossing of tracks should take you towards Eastbourne, rather than Eastdean. It is important here to follow the plinths which mark the route, and make sure you consult a map; the footpath is at this point on a different route. A slippery slope and signpost will bring you out at the car park just below the Links golf course in Eastbourne, in Paradise Drive.

A leaflet on the South Downs Way is available from The Countryside Commission, John Dower House, Crescent Place, Cheltenham, Glos GL50 3RA Tel: (0242) 21381.

A list of accommodation for riders and horses travelling the South Downs Way is available from: Mr Charles Shippam, Laybrook Farm, Goose Green, Pulborough, Sussex RH20 2LN Tel: (07983) 2164. Please send stamped addressed envelope.

9 South Downs Link to Wickham

Mrs V. Jefferies

Approx. 30k, 18.75 miles

OS maps 197, 185, 196

Start: 718182:OS 197
Finish: 573113:OS 196

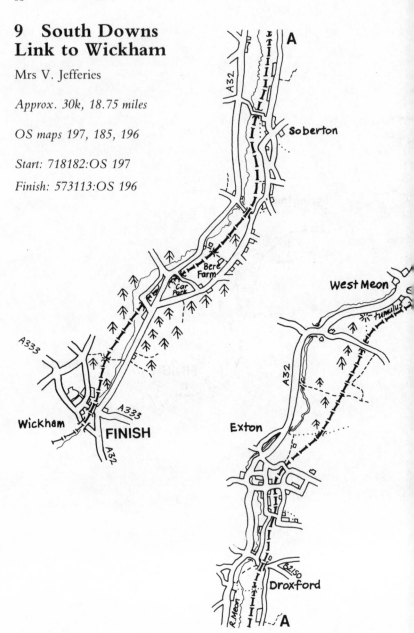

An extension to the west of the South Downs Way. Leave Queen Elizabeth Country Park and cross the A3 (using the underpass); follow tracks to Butser Hill and on to Leythe House where you briefly join the road (turning left) and then take a right onto the bridleway heading north until meeting minor road where you turn right and then take bridleway going left. Tracks and bridleways till you meet the A272, which you must follow (going west) for about a mile before taking side roads to West Meon. Here you pick up the disused railway track, which is now owned by the council and is a permissive route for riders going as far as Wickham.

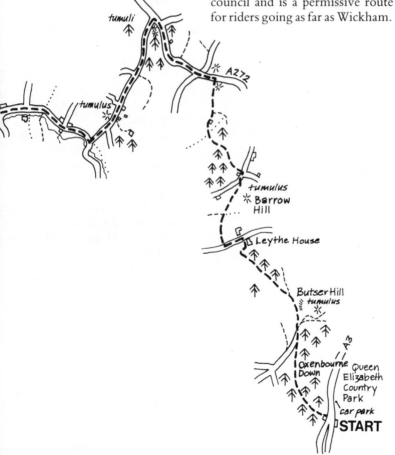

10 New Forest to South Downs Way

Janet M. Boulton

Approx. 100k, 63 miles

OS maps 184, 185, 197

Start: 237237: OS 184

Finish: 718182:OS 197

Commencing at Bramshaw Telegraph on the edge of the New Forest, cross the B3080 and, passing Hope Cottage, continue north-easterly till you can choose either to go west by passing Whiteparish or go east, which involves more roadwork. The westerly route takes you on a left-hand track to Lover where you turn right and, shortly after, left down minor roads. Then a right and almost immediately a left turn brings you to a track which you follow till the T-junction; here turn right going north and ending up at the A36. Cross it and continue over Pepperbox Hill, taking the left-hand fork where the tracks diverge and joining minor road where you turn right and then left going towards East Grimstead.

If going via Whiteparish, proceed from Bramshaw Telegraph due north, till meeting the road where you turn right and then left and follow to Hamptworth; right and right again down a track which will bring you out between some houses on the B2079. Turn left onto the A36, which is a fairly busy road, but fortunately there is a wide grass verge (246219). Take the minor road to Whiteparish after a couple of miles and follow till you come to the church on the A27, where you turn left and then right, following the track to the minor road which takes you west, but then you turn right. You are now on the main route.

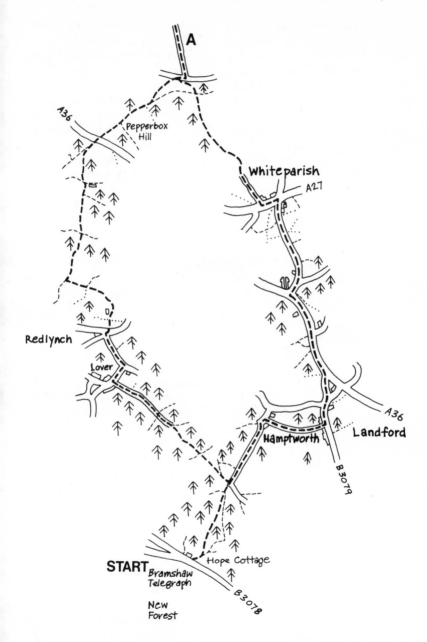

A

A36

Pepperbox
Hill

Whiteparish

A27

Redlynch

Lover

Hamptworth

Landford

A36

B3079

START Bramshaw
Telegraph

Hope Cottage

B3078

New
Forest

Over the railway bridge and continue into East Grimstead following the road north-easterly towards Middle Winterslow until taking a turn on the right (238297). Follow alongside woodland and take the left turn followed shortly by a right turn and another right turn which will bring you out on a minor road on the outskirts of Middle Winterslow. Turn right and right again (248328) onto Roman Road from the Common leading eastwards until you reach Buckholt Farm, where the track takes you off to the left.

This track does a zig-zag to join up again with the Roman Road until nearing Broughton (301316), where you turn left up minor road to B3084 where you turn right and then take track left at Broughton Hill. This track brings you to a road junction at Broughton which you cross and follow the road over a deep ford till it becomes a track.

Anne Steele, a hymn writer, was born in 1717 in Broughton. A

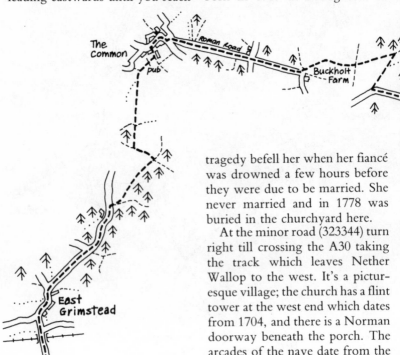

tragedy befell her when her fiancé was drowned a few hours before they were due to be married. She never married and in 1778 was buried in the churchyard here.

At the minor road (323344) turn right till crossing the A30 taking the track which leaves Nether Wallop to the west. It's a picturesque village; the church has a flint tower at the west end which dates from 1704, and there is a Norman doorway beneath the porch. The arcades of the nave date from the 13th century and in the churchyard is a large stone pyramid monument which was erected to

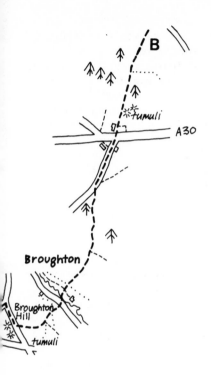

At the road junction cross over and take minor road leading north, then taking track (335380) to the right passing long barrows and arriving at minor road, which again you cross onto track which follows round Hazel Down. This will bring you out on the minor road where you turn left to Fullerton and cross the River Test. Right onto A3057 and then left on bend towards Chilbolton. Turn right and pass a giant telescope which is situated on the right amongst the abandoned runways of a fighter aerodrome which was used during the last war.

Turn left and right and follow minor road to cross A30 where the road becomes a track. Take track on left and follow to B3420, where you turn right and then take path on left to cross A34. This track runs south of South Wonston till meeting minor road where you turn north. Turn right on to track at crossroads, to A33 and Lunways Inn where you cross onto minor road skirting Itchen Wood and turning right on the track travelling southwards along the edge of the wood and passing Lone Farm.

This will bring you to Itchen Abbas going under the railway bridge and taking the road to the left (B3047) and then right to Avington. This takes you through the Itchen Valley and past Avington; Avington Church was built during the 3 years following 1768.

the memory of a member of the Douce family in 1760. Further on, Danebury Hill is on your left. The fort is a fine example of an Iron Age camp which has been thoroughly excavated in recent years, during which a gold plated Gallo Belgic coin was found which was in good condition; it is unlikely that it was dropped much after 70 BC. There are massive earthworks, circular ditches and banks round the hill top which enclose approximately 13 acres. From the hill fort are excellent views of the surrounding countryside.

It is brick built and has a fine marble monument to the Marchioness of Carnarvon. Pass Avington Manor Farm and cross the A31. This track takes you over Gander Down. To the east is Cheriton, where a battle was fought during the Civil War. On March 28th, 1644, the Cavaliers, under Lord Hopton, who had been quartered at Winchester, were massed on the high ground south of Alresford. The Roundheads, led by Sir William Waller, were on the long ridge north of Hinton Ampner. Each army consisted of about 10,000 men. During the morning the battle commenced, and by nightfall the Cavaliers were defeated. So heavy were the losses that the lanes are said 'to have run with blood'. The king's cause never recovered from this defeat.

Cross the A272 passing Holding Farm and continuing south to pass Mill Barrows (597238). Continue on minor road until turning left on bridleway (598227) towards Warnford. Turn right into Warnford, passing Warnford Park, which contains two structures of interest: the ruins of a building known as King John's House, which dates from about 1230, and the parish church. The church is largely Norman; it was rebuilt by Adam de Port who held Warnford from 1171 till 1213 when he died. It contains two early 17th-century monuments to members of the Neale family, one of which bears the full-length figures of Sir Thomas Neale and his two wives with the figures of their children.

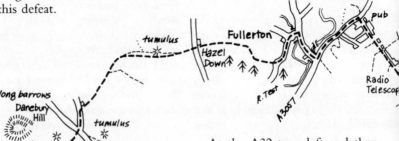

At the A32 turn left and then take minor road on the right, then crossing road onto track (645217) passing north-east of Old Winchester Hill. This is a beauty spot which lies approximately 12 miles east of Winchester, one of a chain of ancient strongholds which stretched across Hampshire. Only

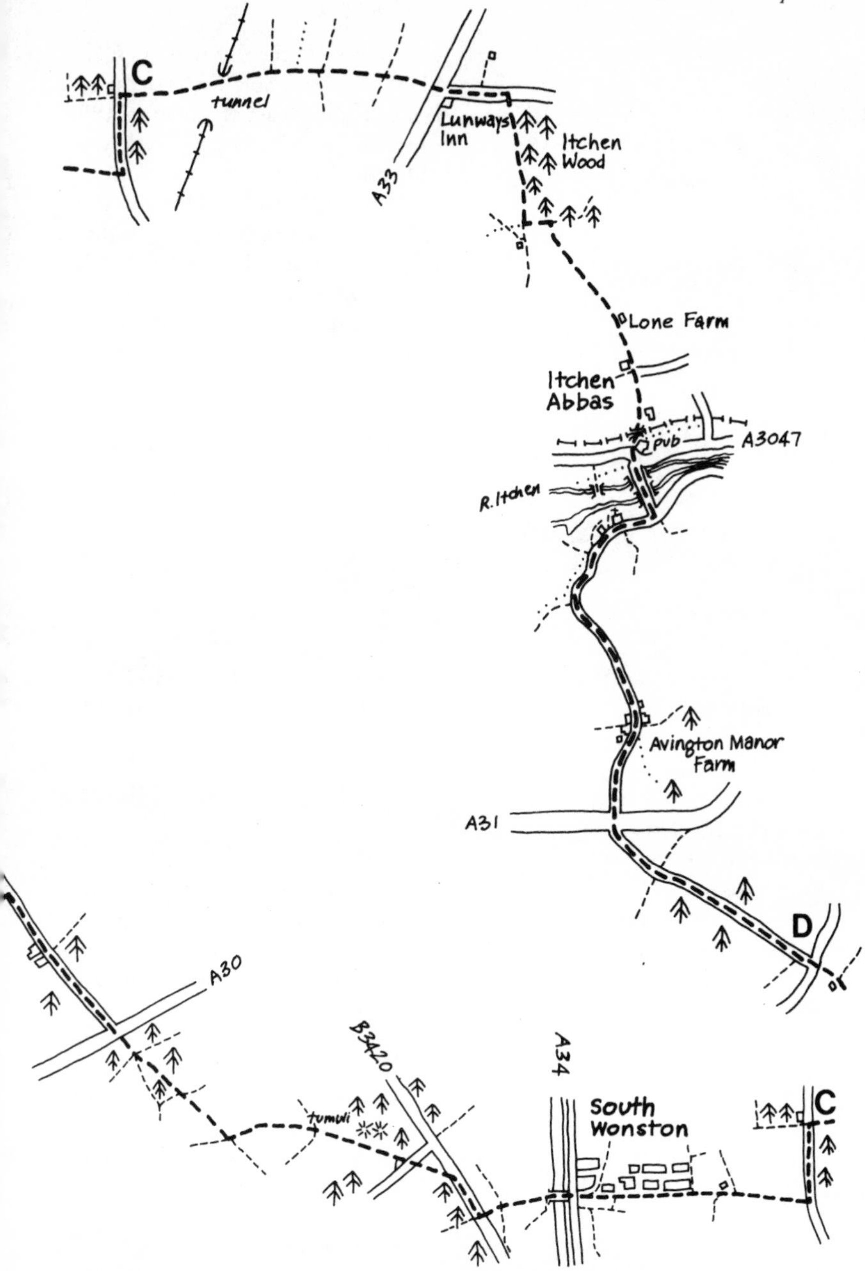

C

tunnel

A33

Lunways Inn

Itchen Wood

Lone Farm

Itchen Abbas

pub

A3047

R. Itchen

Avington Manor Farm

A31

D

A30

B3420

A34

tumuli

South Wonston

C

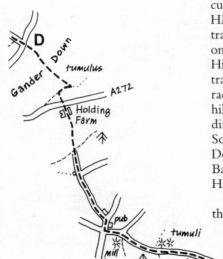

cury over Wether Down. Left in
HMS Mercury and at 684189 take
track leading east from map 185
onto map 197. Over Tegdown
Hill and Hyden Hill and follow
track towards Butser Hill and the
radio tower. From the top of this
hill there are excellent views in all
directions – to the south is the
Solent, to the east are the South
Downs, to the north is the Hogs
Back and to the west is the Plain of
Hampshire.

Take track to the south passing
the reconstructed Iron Age Farm-

part of the ancient earthworks
now survives.

Turn left through Whitewood
and then turn right towards
Coombe where you turn left onto
minor road. This brings you out
at Coombe Cross; north-east lies
East Meon, where there is a
splendid Norman church renowned for its architecture. The
nave, transepts and arches sup-
porting the tower and spire date
from about 1130, the south aisle
and south chapel date from the
following century and the chancel
from the fifteenth century. It contains one of four fonts in Hampshire which is carved in tournai
marble.

Take track towards HMS Mer-

stead. This is the work of the
Butser Ancient Farm Research
Project consisting of a thatched
round house in its own enclosure
as well as other farm buildings.
Use underpass to travel to east side
of the A3 which will bring you to
Queen Elizabeth Country Park
which extends for 1,400 acres.
Keep to bridlepaths here and
follow north-eastwards emerging
through bridle gate (734198) onto
South Downs Way.

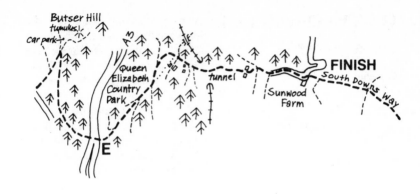

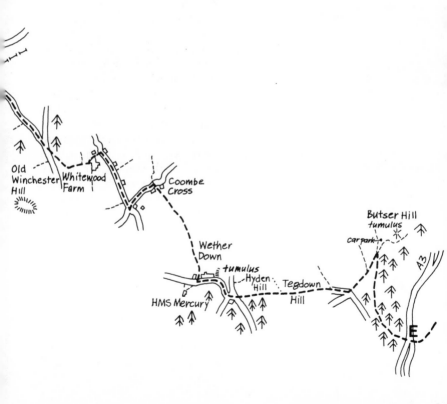

11 The Downs Link

Approx. 48k, 30 miles

OS maps 186, 187, 198

Start: 032483:OS 186

Finish: 194094:OS 198

A footpath and bridleway that joins the North and South Downs Ways. It is well marked at each end and follows mainly the track of a disused railway line. It leaves the North Downs Way at St Martha's Hill, west of Guildford and just east of St Martha's 11th-century church. It is waymarked down to the Tillingbourne Valley, passing Lockner Farm riding stables and crossing the busy A248. Straight across the road, past cottages and over railway bridge. Having passed house on right, cross a track and follow right-hand fork on to Blackheath. Then on down a sandy track and cross Sample Oak Lane.

Join a metalled road and pass Great Tangley Manor on your right. Signpost indicates bridleway avoiding the B2128, then straight across the road onto a track leading to Chinthurst Hill. Car park on your right, then turn sharp right across agricultural land. Shortly you will turn left and follow on down to the minor road by Chinthurst Farm. Cross this road and join the route down to the railway track on the verge. Turn south and follow the track (though a detour has been made because a bridge was demolished). Then you go onto the remains of an aqueduct which used to carry the Wey and Arun canal over the river. In Bramley you cross the road just south of the station and continue behind houses until

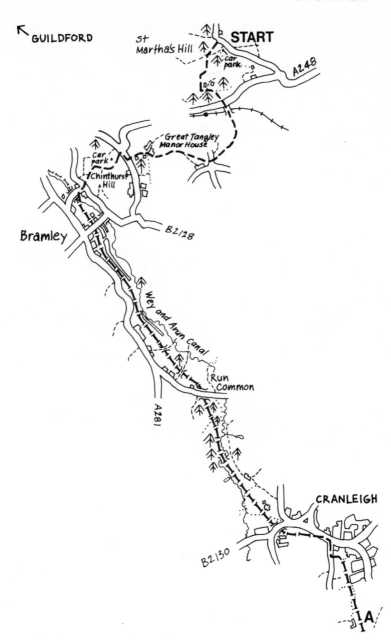

GUILDFORD

St Martha's Hill

START

car park

A248

Great Tangley Manor House

Car park

Chinthurst Hill

Bramley

B2128

Wey and Arun Canal

Run Common

A281

CRANLEIGH

B2130

A

reaching open country again.

The Wey and Arun Canal (now defunct) runs beside the route here. On to Run Common, an open common so called because gypsies used to graze their ponies here. Onto sheet 187 towards Cranleigh, where you must leave the route because the station has been built over. Turn left and cross Cranleigh Common, then turn right into the High St. Right into Knowle Lane, and take care, since this is narrow and busy. Left at the signpost and you are back on the old railway track. Then, in a few miles, you come to Baynards Station, now a private residence. The pub, the Thurlow Arms, was built by a former owner of Baynards Manor, who allowed the railway to cross his land. Keeping the station on your left, turn left along the road and then right, back onto the track (gates of Baynards Manor nearby with formal drive). After the road bridge has crossed the route, you must turn left and left again to cross the bridge. Then on the left you will find a signpost to the bridleway which goes through South Wood; a new surface has been put down here

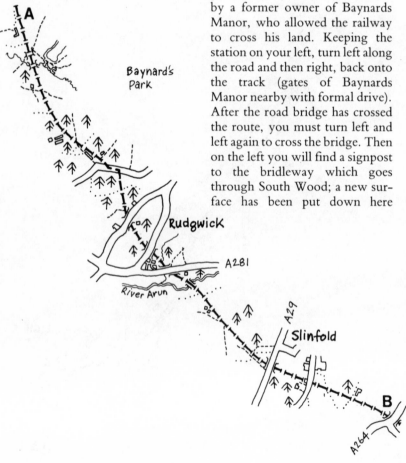

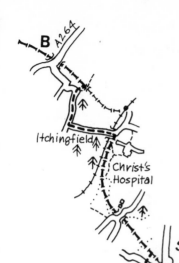

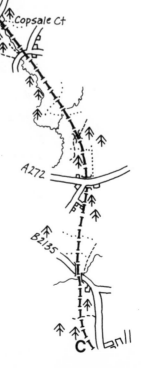

Continue in a south-easterly direction, go under the A264 and, in just under half a mile, you leave the railway track. Turn north-east to Mill Lane, cross over the bridge and follow Mill Lane and the Fulfords Road in the direction of Itchingfield. The church of St Nicolas is part-Norman and has a 600-year-old belfry tower of oak, and a curious 15th-century half-timbered priest's house in the churchyard which was used by

because the soil is heavy clay. Rhododendrons grow over the county boundary bank, which you pass through before turning left and descending a ramp back onto the track. Continue south along ramp and join railway track in 100 yards.

Through Rudgwick and cross the A281 (busy) and then the River Arun (unusual two-tiered bridge – two having been built because the railway inspector disliked the steep gradient to Rudgwick Station). Pass through various sidings and cuttings and on to Slinfold where you cross the A29, an old Roman Road, Stane Street, which connected London to Chichester.

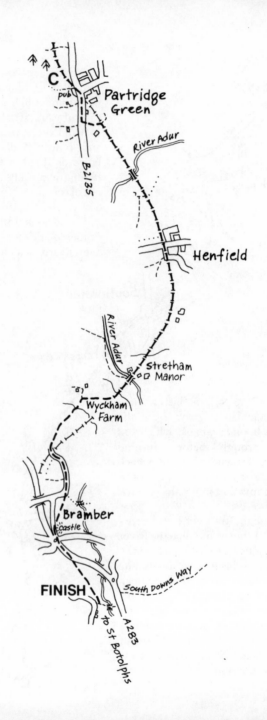

monks of Sele Priory, Upper Beeding, when they came to collect their dues.

Turn left into Christ's Hospital Rd, and in half a mile you will see the famous Bluecoat School. The route continues alongside the main Horsham railway line, and you rejoin the track at Itchingfield Junction. Carry on to Southwater, where there is a slight diversion along a temporary route south-west of the cutting. Then go south-west along a track towards the church, follow the bridleway towards the village and go down Church Lane and Andrews Lane to the west of the telephone exchange, at which point you turn north-east and rejoin the track. You will have to negotiate the A24. A little further on, you join the metal road again at Station Rd, at the end of which you turn right into Cripplegate Lane and almost immediately left to a farm road, where you rejoin the railway track (and onto map 198).

You now pass through some glorious countryside; on the left you can see Copsale Court; further down the track is West Grimstead Station, with the old platforms still in existence. At 190190 you leave the track again, go over the bridge on the B2135 and continue on this road until turning left just outside Partridge Green into a farm access road bringing you back to the railway track. Now

you are getting into Weald country with views of the downs and the spire of St Hugh's Monastery to the east. Cross the River Adur and go through a deep cutting to come out at Henfield, where the path again makes a short diversion to the east leaving the track near the police station and rejoining it along Station Rd. Just outside Henfield is Stretham Manor on your left, where the Romans crossed the River Adur in the first century. (A mile to the east is Woods Mill, an old water mill now the headquarters of the Sussex Trust of Nature Conservation. However, the path to it is only a footpath.)

Ahead, and to the west, you can see Chanctonbury Rings on the crest of the downs. Just after Stretham Manor, the path leaves the railway and you go up a ramp to the top of the cutting and over a field just north of Wyckham Farm. Left onto metal road and south for half a mile, crossing the railway track. Via Kings Barn Lane, Kingstone Avenue and Castle Lane, and you reach the roundabout at Bramber Castle. Now owned by the National Trust, the castle is a Norman fortress built in 1083; it used to be the home of the de Braose family, and was built on the former course of the River Adur. All that is left after it was destroyed during the Civil War is part of the keep and the earthworks. A Norman church is also on the same hill.

You must now follow the Bramber/Steyning by-pass on the verge until rejoining the railway track and going southwards to meet the South Downs Way just north of St Botolph's church.

A guide to the Downs Link can be purchased from any of the local authorities responsible for its development. Their addresses and telephone numbers are given below:

West Sussex County Council
County Hall, Chichester
West Sussex PO19 1RL
Tel: (0243) 777100

Waverley Borough Council
The Burys, Godalming
Surrey KT1 2DN
Tel: (04868) 4104

Surrey County Council
County Hall, Penrhyn Road
Kingston-upon-Thames
Surrey GU7 1HR
Tel: (01) 546 1050

12 Part of the North Downs Way
(Dorking to Guildford: St Martha's Hill Section)

Sheila Beardall

Approx. 19k, 12 miles

OS maps 186, 187

Start: 170520:OS 187

Finish: 004485:OS 186

Unfortunately not all the North Downs Way is a bridleway. But there is a lovely stretch covering about 12 miles from Ranmore, above Dorking, going east to Guildford, which is open to riders.

Since the way is a long-distance footpath and only 24 miles south of central London it can become busy in sunny weather. But much of the track is wide enough to give plenty of leeway to both walkers and riders. The only real congestion tends to occur at Newlands Corner, above Guildford. In the summer this lovely stretch of grassland attracts hordes of picnickers and kite-flyers.

The way passes mainly through woodland and there are numerous bridleways leading off which are worth investigating.

It is also possible to ride a circuit of about 35 miles by striking south from Newlands Corner to Blackheath and following the string of bridleways leading over Winterfold, Pitch Hill, Hurtwood, Holmbury Hill and Leith Hill before turning north to rejoin the North Downs Way at Ranmore.

There is practically no road work involved. But good map reading and a compass are essential as these wonderful Surrey Hills are unexpectedly empty, except around the car parks. They are also heavily wooded and dissected by fire breaks which can quickly cause disorientation.

It is possible to ride further east

than this section by crossing the A24 by Burford Bridge Hotel and riding over Box Hill and towards Reigate. But to the west North Downs Way and Pilgrims Way cross the River Wey south of Guildford by a ferry or foot-bridges which are not rideable.

Riders can either start out from the large public car park at the foot of Box Hill or park up on Ranmore Common where there is also plenty of space. If starting from below Box Hill you have to cross the A24 dual carriageway. But there are wide verges and you are immediately in the delightful village of West Humble, which boasts several pubs. Once through the village, there is a bridleway to the left opposite Chapel Farm leading up through Ashcombe Wood to meet the lane to Ranmore.

There are wide grassy verges which lead to the top of the North Downs and then carry on around to the right to follow the road which runs along the top. This is a well used track and the main peril is other galloping horses!

To the right are other tempting tracks leading to Polesden Lacey and Fetcham Downs. But riders aiming to join the North Downs Way must keep level with the road for as long as possible and then cross it, but keep as near to the top of the downs as they can, in order to join the official Way at Dog-kennel Green. The track carries on through dense woods keeping fields in sight on the right and occasional glimpses over the Surrey Hills to the left. It crosses a lane which leads up from the A25 east of Abinger Hammer.

Soon after the crossing the way veers slightly left away from the fields and through the woods to come out above Hackhurst Downs. There are bridleways to the right which lead eventually to Effingham Forest, but the criss-cross of paths can be confusing.

A wide gravelly track continues

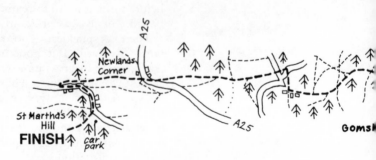

along the top of the downs above Gomshall and Shere (where there is a blacksmith) until passing through a farm. Keep to the right-hand driveway which joins a lane. Turn right and almost immediately left over a very short bridleway to cross another lane. The way continues on the other side through dense woods on softer going until emerging into the light once more on the side of the A25. Opposite is Newlands Corner, a famous beauty spot, with wonderful views towards the coast and a large car park. The way leads over the A25, slightly right and across the top of the hill to join White Lane.

Turn sharp left down a steep hill and below are a variety of very sandy tracks leading up and over St Martha's Hill.

Once at the top of St Martha's there is the choice of riding along the combined North Downs Way and Pilgrims Way into the outskirts of Guildford or turning south to meet the A248, and perhaps following the previous Downs Link route. Parking is difficult in either case, but there are two car parks on either side of St Martha's Hill.

Another alternative is to cross the A248 east of Chilworth and take the bridleway opposite which goes over a railway bridge. This leads to Blackheath which has a large car park, a pub and some superb sandy gallops.

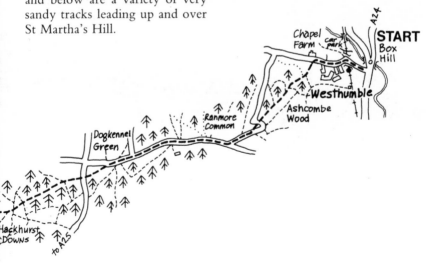

13 Old Alresford Pond to Danebury Hill

Sam Hart

Approx. 33½k, 21 miles

OS map 185

Start: 576334:OS 185

Finish: 324377:OS 185

This route takes you through the mid-Hampshire heartland, following an ancient route called the Lunway, which was once thought to be an ancient route from London to Old Sarum and was referred to in Saxon charters as a 'herepath', a warrior's path, safe for a skirmishing party wishing to keep away from Roman roads and villages. The name derives from the Saxon 'Leodi' or public way and probably existed even before the Saxons.

The bridleway starts on the west side of Old Alresford Pond, but in less than half a mile you need to turn south to join a minor road, another half a mile further on. Go west on this road, until, after half a mile, you turn west onto a trackway (572336) to join

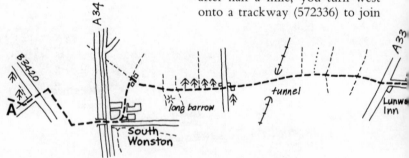

the Wayfarers Walk (Emsworth to Inkpen Beacon). Follow this Wayfarers Walk north-west till in a mile you reach a cross track near three barrows. Ahead are two diverging tracks. Choose the north-east one rather than the north-north-east one. Follow this track north-west up across Itchen Stoke Down, past the trig point at the summit before descending to the minor road which leads you west to the Lunways Inn. Here you have to cross the busy A33 trunk road from Winchester to the M3; you are advised to dismount and wait patiently until a lull in the traffic allows you to cross safely. Experience has shown that the best time to cross busy trunk roads is before 8 a.m. and after 6 p.m. in summer, or during the midday break, 1 p.m. to 2 p.m., when a lot of lorry drivers pull up for lunch.

Once across the A33 remount and follow the Lunway westward across the countryside, past another trig point where the London-Winchester railway passes in a tunnel underneath until you reach the northern edge of South Wonston. Here it is best to turn south through South Wonston (465366) before turning west again to cross the dual carriageway of the A34 by the newly built bridge. After crossing the bridge you soon turn north parallel to the B3420 which, by turning southwest, you will cross onto the minor road to Crawley. At the first farm buildings down this road, turn north-west (434360) – sometimes there is an iron gate to negotiate – and follow this track till in 1½ miles on the north side of a belt of trees you come to a crossways. Ahead the track points west-south-west but you make a right-angled turn to follow the track going north-west until you come to the A30. To the north of

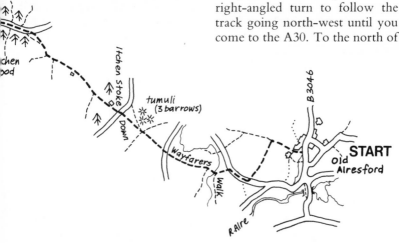

this track lies Brockley Warren, a Nature Conservancy site of special scientific interest. This was farmed for rabbits after the 1838 Tithe Survey, but was nearly lost as a chalk grassland in 1940; it is now populated with chalk and flowers, butterflies and birds.

Cross the A30 and take the minor road down to Chilbolton. In Chilbolton you have a choice: you can follow the village street south-westerly, past the Bishops Mitre, until you can turn north down Joy Lane onto Chilbolton Common, where a bridleway takes you north to the far west end of Wherwell. This bridleway fords two or three sections of the River Test, alongside narrow foot-bridges. The one nearest Wherwell necessitates 50 yards of wading, and although the bottom is firm gravel, the rider needs to pick the shallowest route. If your horses are not ready for this minor adventure you are advised to follow the road route to Wherwell called Ghost Walk, where, after a great slaughter between King Stephen and the Empress Matilda's troops in 1141, deserters from King Stephen's army were hung from a corner tree. On this route you can appreciate the lovely village of Wherwell, especially if you turn down the lane by the War Memorial leading to the church. This lane must be one of the loveliest in Hampshire, with cottages like a dream world.

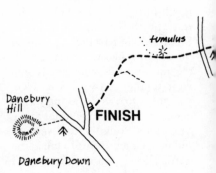

Back on your road through the village, follow the signpost to Fullerton, at the White Lion, until you come to the A3057. Turn south on this for 300 yards and turn west onto a minor road across a river bridge and immediately south onto another minor road before at a sharp right-hand bend, a bridleway straight ahead leads you onto the last 3 miles to Danebury. After all this road-work, there are lovely wide grassy tracks, inviting you to a final gallop up to the Iron Age Fort. Danebury is the best chronicled Iron Age Fort in Hampshire, with ample car parks, whose history has been well chronicled by Professor Barry Cunliffe.

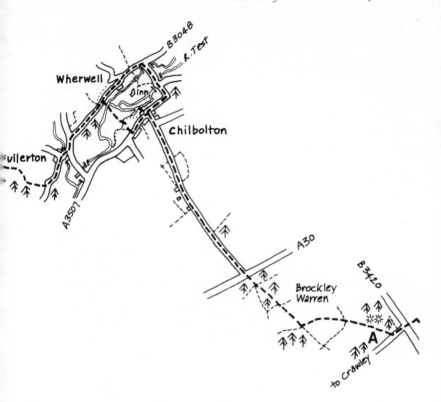

14 Watership Down to the River Avon and Old Sarum

Sam Hart

Approx. 73k, 45 miles

OS maps 174, 185, 184

Start: 516567:OS 174

Finish: 138327:OS 184

This route starts at Watership Down, made famous by the eponymous book about rabbits and is well marked by logo WW (Wayfarer's Way) along the escarpment of the North Hampshire Downs. The route sweeps south through Collingbourne Wood, bypasses the military camps at Derham and Tidworth by using the plain and then turns south again to join the Avon at Great Durnford which it follows to Old Sarum.

At Great Durnford the rider may cross the Avon at a weir near the Black Horse and follow a bridlepath to Lake, where another bridlepath goes west and north to Springbottom and on to Normanton Down, which is the best approach to Stonehenge that a visitor could have.

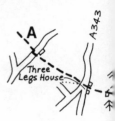

Starting on White Hill south of Kingsclere, you are immediately in the land of the horse, with beautiful downs and gallops on both sides of you as you travel westward. Open downs, of thick green grass; the Watership down rabbits cannot be as greedy as those on Salisbury Plain and the first fence not for $1\frac{1}{2}$ miles, a horse-rider's heaven. At this fence a WW logo directs you to a wicket gate and the path takes you to cross a minor road. For the adventurous there are even some jumps beside the path. Across the minor road, you pass off the track through an iron gate and follow the tractor tyre marks north and then west to another gate (the map is at fault here). At the second gate the track follows the hedge south, but in 100 yards a right angle turn

takes you to Ladle Hill, another Iron Age Fort. Keep to the south side of Ladle Hill and outside the boundary fence before swinging off south-west to join the track for Great Litchfield Down. Here are glorious views of Beacon Hill on the west side of the A34. As you come off Great Litchfield Down, navigate through the plantations and under the electricity grid wires to yet another gate in a little valley. Ahead, through the archway of a disused railway, lies the dual carriageway of the A34. You are advised to dismount and patiently await your turn in crossing this busy road. Again, lunchtime is the quietest period to cross.

Once across, follow the track westward, climbing up above Highclere Stud and crossing the A343 at Three Legs House, now a private residence, but once a pub, from which spare horses were hitched on to pull waggons up the steep hill from Newbury. Your way now leads in a sweep along the escarpment all the way to Inkpen Hill and Combe Gibbet, although for ¼ mile a minor road spoils the rhythm of your trot. At the Gibbet (still standing) not only are there views north across the Kennet Vale but southward across the rolling downs of North Hampshire. In 2 miles you cross a minor road from Buttermere to Ham, but push on westward for another 1½ miles to another road junction from Shalbourne which forks to either Oxenwood or Fosbury. Take the south-west road to Oxenwood 1¾ miles away. Oxenwood is publess and shopless but has a pleasant green, which serves as a road junction. Take the south-west Tidcombe Road, but in 100 yards turn south on a hard road to Beacon Farm. South of this

farm a pleasant grass track leads over Haydown Hill and down to Hippenscombe (where you have to go right through the farmyard) before climbing steeply to Chute Causeway (the only Roman Road with a big curve).

Now unfortunately your route is in a small corner of map 185, which you soon leave for map 184. So from Chute Causeway travel south for ¾ mile and then a right-angled turn west takes you to Upper Chute, reached after crossing a minor road, which leads to Chute Standon, Lower Chute and Chute Cadley. So beware. Upper Chute is the only one with a church, but you need to find the Cross Keys (which does a good pub lunch) on a road out of the village leading west. Just past the Cross Keys, a track leads you south to Honey Bottom. A single cottage in Honey Bottom is where you look for a track south-west up a rise into Collingbourne Forest and onto map 184. There are many tracks in the woods, but travelling south-west for a mile you will reach a track junction where you swing west, until you pick up a hard track taking you west, then south to Blackmore Down, past a farmyard called Pig Henge on the south-west corner of the forest.

Turn west here and in a mile pass under a railway tunnel, before emerging onto a road fork on the A342. Ahead of you is MoD land and barbed wire, but a hunt gate in

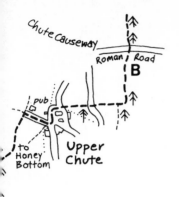

the wire points the way to the open country ahead. Unfortunately this is sometimes strip grazed, and ringed with an electric fence. The gate also is a bit of a problem. If necessary switch off the electric fence unit, find where the cattle are driven in and out and switch on the fence again when clear. Other times you can ride round the outside of the electric fence, and legally it should not obstruct the bridleway.

However, follow the track westward which passes north of Windmillhill, till you reach the A338. Cross over where there is slight diversion past some cottages and still ride west, keeping to the north side of the military cemetery. In one mile you will be up on the wild plain, with Sidbury Iron Age camp to the south of you. In $\frac{1}{2}$ mile you turn south, along a short section of the Old Marlborough Rd but indistinguishable from all the other tracks, unless you spot the single

milestone sticking out on the downs.

Your destination is Dunch Hill and the beech and fir belt along its ridge. The direction is south-east. Too far east and you will see Tidworth Barracks, too far west and you will find yourself down in Bourne Bottom, so keep to the high ground.

When you reach the beech and fir belt of Dunch Hill your track follows the Wilts/Herts boundary, all the way south-east to the Tidworth–Bulford road, which you cross at the Cross Belt. The bridleway, now you have left the plain, runs between high hedges to the western edge of Shipton Bellinger, and at an old beech tree, known locally as 'The Beech Tree' here at a crossways, turn south-west. This is the old drove road from Shipton Bellinger to Salisbury and is easy to follow for the next 3 miles, on across the A303 road, and a minor road. Once across the minor road follow the belt of trees out to the next minor road which leads to Arundel Farm, as the correct bridleway is blocked with bushes.

At Arundel Farm, you can pick up the original bridlepath, but you soon come to yet another minor road and ahead the main runway of Boscombe Down Airfield. The old drove road was right down the middle of this runway, before the war. Now you must follow the old railway cutting west and out-

side the airfield perimeter fence
until you come to the edge of the
airmen's quarters and meet the
Old Marlborough Rd again. (If
going in the opposite direction,
there is a green sign to Allington
just before the railway bridge; go
down behind fence and beside
perimeter fence of airfield.) This
track is fairly overgrown. A
right-angled turn to the south-
west takes you up to the Guard
Room, then follow a road, still
south-west (with a wide verge).
Until a sharp bend takes this road
west, whilst you continue south-
west along a track to join the A345
Salisbury–Amesbury road.

Luckily you don't have to go
along this busy road, but ride
along a track beside the airfield
landing lights parallel to the road.
Look out for overgrown cattle
grids at each end. At the end of the
landing lights on a minor road,
turn north-west, cross the A345,
negotiate a gate and a pleasant
track leads you down to Great
Durnford.

Now follows 4 miles of
roadwork down the side of the
River Avon to Stratford Sub
Castle and Old Sarum (to which
you will not be admitted by the
custodian, who tells you to 'remove horses from the monument'
– because of fouling!). The minor
road on the east side of the Avon is
the quietest. (You can turn east at
Little Durnford down a track, and
then south, to avoid the road.)

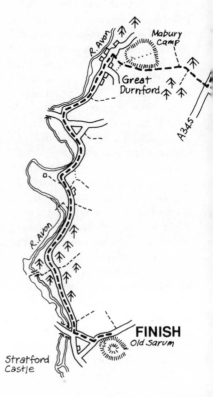

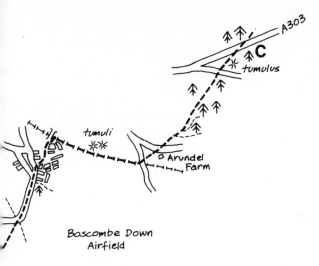

A303

C

tumulus

tumuli

Arundel
Farm

Boscombe Down
Airfield

15 The Kerry Ridgeway

Approx. 25k, 15½ miles

OS maps 136, 137

Start: 109848:OS 136

Finish: 323892:OS 137

Otherwise known as 'The Castle Road', the Kerry Ridgeway is a bridleway and open to horses from Cider House Farm to Bishops Castle. It is a pleasant ride across the Kerry hills, with good views and passing some interesting archaeological sites. The route is not difficult to follow. Going west to east, you first cross Cross Dyke, built by the builders of

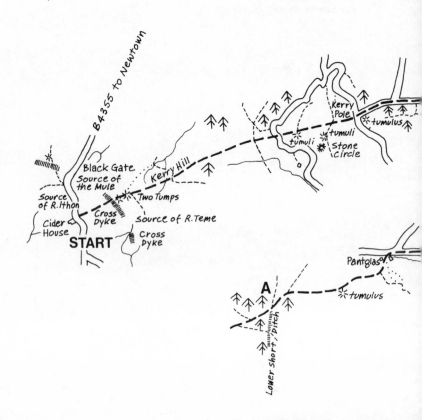

Offa's Dyke; then you pass the Two Tumps, or tumuli, two of the seven that lie beside the path. Further on you cross Upper Short Ditch and Lower Short Ditch, both probably built by Iron Age peoples to mark boundaries.

At 203871 (OS 137) lies the Cantlin Stone. There are various suggestions about its origins: it could be derived from 'Cant Tell'

Stone; another story has it that a traveller died whilst walking the Ridgeway; the responsibility for burying him was a matter of contention between parishes of Kerry and Bettws-y-Crwyn, and finally the latter buried him. The stone was erected where the body was found.

Offa's Dyke itself crosses the route at 258897 and, just east of it lies Caer Din Ring, a defensive settlement of the Iron Age.

Just before reaching Bishops Castle you pass Bishopsmoat motte and bailey, a large bailey and a 27-foot high motte.

A helpful leaflet on the Kerry Ridgeway is available from Planning Information Service, Powys County Council, Llandrindod Wells.

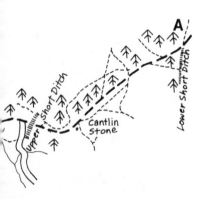

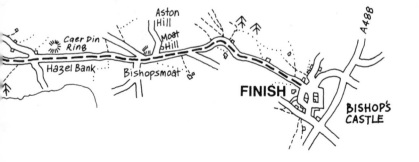

16 Two circular routes near Forest of Brechfa

Lesley Gibbons

Approx. 80k, 50 miles

OS map 146

Start: 507348:OS 146

Leaving Blue Well ride north-west across mountain to boundary fence. Cross road and continue near fence to 2nd cattle grid. Through gate and along road for $\frac{1}{4}$ mile. Turn left and ride parallel to road on grass. Follow track, passing farm on left. Continue on track across moor to Bwlch-y-Clawdd Farm Continue, keeping fence on left, then bear right following track to negotiate gulley. Follow grass track to road. Cross over, turn left and ride on moor near to road. Down steep bank and across stream and join Nant-y-Hendre farm track. Continue past farm keeping fence on left to mountain gate.

Follow track to stream and continue until track ends at farm gate. Swing 90° right and follow Land Rover track to road. Left across bridge (slippery tarmac), ride on grass to left of road and follow track. Straight across at crossroads and continue to cattle grid. Through gate and along road through village. Turn left at Banc Farm Lane and immediately left into forestry.

Bear left and left again down steep track. Left at the bottom along forestry road then right at next junction and right again to Trawscoed. Bear right between cottages then left along forestry road. Turn sharp right along path up steep bank and right again at top. Follow forestry road, keeping left at crossroads, and right at T junction. Sharp right into plantation and follow grassy path through trees. Rejoin forestry road and bear right. Left at fork and immediately turn left down steep path. (Alternatively continue along forestry road keeping left until you rejoin route at foot of path.) Turn left and follow track by stream to bridge.

Cross bridge and follow road uphill. Right at the top then right along path at bend in road. Follow path through plantation, then right at forestry road and turn right into Banc Farm field. Water troughs. Through gate at top right-hand corner onto farm road and bear right going towards Llidiadnenog. Turn right into forestry and continue along track.

Through village to cattle grid. Turn sharp left and ride across moor to boundary fence. Follow path to road. Cross over and follow farm road. Down steep hill (take care) and cross stream. Bear right up steep bank then turn left, keeping fence on left. Continue straight on at corner of field, ride across open moor to fence. Follow track to right. Sharp left then ride on grass to right of track down to stream. Cross and follow sheep track to left. Continue on moor following stream valley, then bear right following telegraph poles to Bryn Llewelyn and turn right along track. Ford stream then bear left up gulley. Join track, then follow path across open moor back to road. Turn left and continue to cattle grid. Keep on moor to left of road until you reach Blue Well lane, and back to venue.

Second loop: Start as for previous route, but at road turn left through gate by first cattle grid. Ride along path by trees to edge of forestry, then turn left along fence. Sharp left into forest then right after fallen tree and follow path to road. Left to gate then right along path by fence. Sharp left and follow path to forestry road. Turn right then bear left at fork and turn sharp left into path. Turn left and then right at junctions, cross over forestry road and continue along path until forestry road is rejoined. Turn right following road around valley then right at next fork.

Straight across at T junction along path. Bear right under trees. Please take care, low branches. Keep right along path by fence. There are deep ruts in this path so keep in single file and take care. Continue along stony path down hill to forestry road, keep right.

Bear left after $\frac{3}{4}$ mile and follow path to stream.

Left across stream and continue along forestry track. Right at junction and right again at fork. Left up stony track then bear right towards Cwymyronnen Uchaf. Right along forestry track, then bear left and continue past farm fields. Bear right at fork, then continue straight on at crossroads. Left at T junction, then bear right and follow forestry road.

Then retrace route, but instead of turning· left up grass track continue along forestry road. Left at junction and continue to crossroads. Turn left along track and bear right at fork. Continue to forestry road, then straight across to rejoin path and retrace route back to Blue Well.

Mrs Lesley Gibbons of Blue Well Riding Centre, Ffynnonlas, Llanllwni, Dyfed Tel: (026 789) 274, provided this route. The Blue Well can supply their own horses, or can put up yours.

17 Two circular routes near Cheltenham

Mrs Pamela Gormley

Approx. 80k, 50 miles

OS map 163

Start: 974243:OS 163

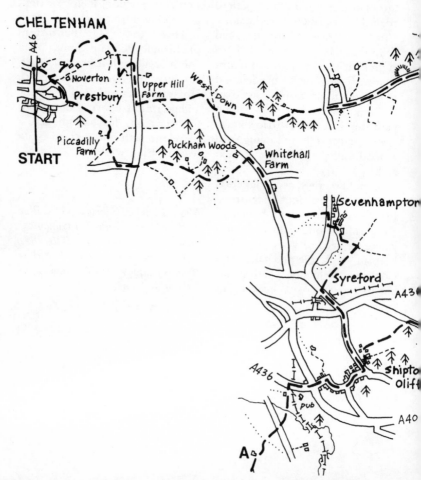

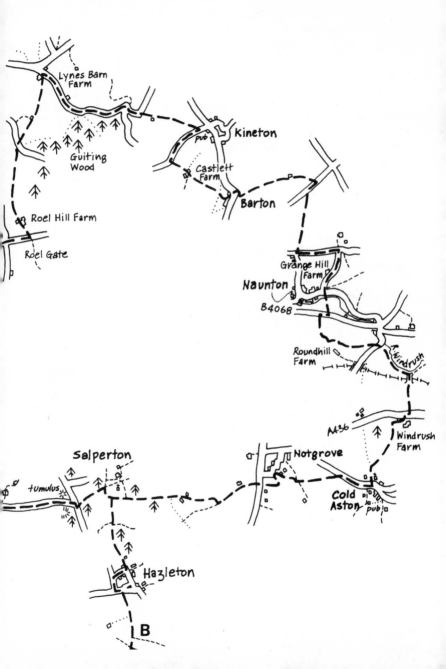

This was used as a Golden Horse-shoe Ride and provides a good hard ride over hilly country with plenty of Cotswold stone.

Start at A46, turn left at road junction, follow track up hill to the end, bear right. Past Upper Hill Farm, take track on left to West Down and east to Roel Gate. Over crossroads turn left, past Roel Hill Farm to Lynes Barn. Turn right along lane, through Guiting Wood nearly to Kineton. Right down lane, left through Castlett Farm to Barton and up track. On road turn south along track to Grange Hill, left then right down through Naunton.

Cross B4068 toward Roundhill Farm, follow stream past Lower Harford, cross disused railway, over A436 through Windrush Farm to Cold Aston (was called Aston Blank). Turn west to Notgrove, Salperton Park and Shipton. Through Shipton Oliffe and over A40 to Frog Mill Inn.

Leave up track past cricket ground over road, past Shill Hill, quickly over two lanes and on through Withington Woods and onto road; turn right, bridleway on left brings you to road passing Stowell Park. Bridleway to left to Hampnett, left along green lane for 1 mile then north to Hazleton and Salperton Park.

For 2½ miles repeat course, short of Shipton turn right by Electricity Station, north over A436, right up track short of

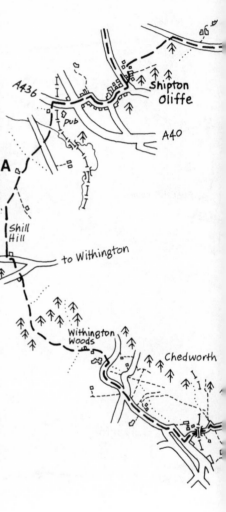

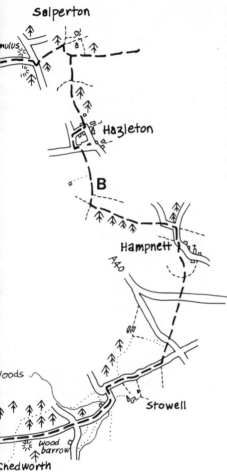

Syreford, in 1 mile left through small gate by covert, down into Sevenhampton, through ford, right then left on top road, up hill through fields, right on road, in 1 mile left down track, in 2nd field follow track to right through Puckham Wood.

Straight on, one field over cross lanes, bear right through Piccadilly and down deep track to Noverton, and A46.

18 Clare to Kettlebaston

Pauline Cutler

Approx. 30k, 19 miles

OS map 155

Start: 777448:OS 155

Finish: 959498:OS 155

This route starts at the bottom of Hickford Hill where there is room to park on the verge. Take the cinder track by the bridlepath sign, do a dog leg on an arable field, onto a narrow little path and continue straight through Bower Hall to the road at Pentlow Church. Follow the road straight on, round a couple of bends until you reach the dairy farm at Pentlow Street. There may be gates to open and shut there.

Continue along the bridlepath to the next section of road, straight on to Weston Hall. Go down the hill, round several bends, past the chemical works, and up the hill to Liston Church. Turn left and follow the lane over the River Stour, turn left and right into St Catherine's Road, and finally into the main street of Long Melford.

This would be a good place for refreshment, possibly at the Cock and Bell. Turn left and go north up the street – the Cock and Bell is on

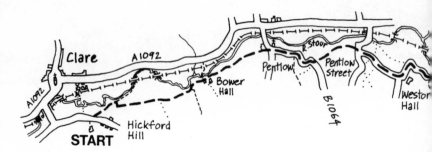

the left – go over the River Chad, having passed The Bull on your right, and have a gallop up the green keeping to the left. Cross the road by the Black Lion, and continue across the next piece of green, onto the Bury St Edmunds road for a short distance. By the Hare, cross the road and into an entrance signposted bridlepath, through a Garden Centre, up a concrete road, and at the top onto a cart track, following the signs to Lavenham. The alternative is to go right in Long Melford and turn left up disused railway.

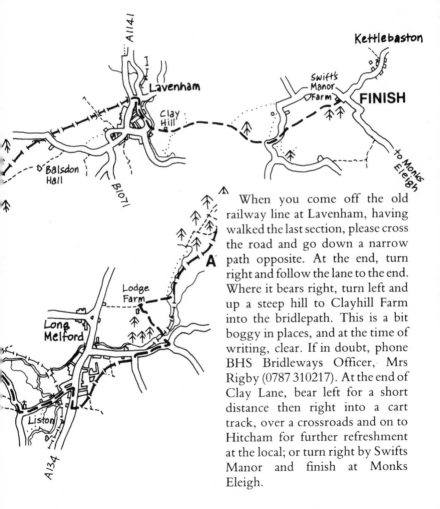

When you come off the old railway line at Lavenham, having walked the last section, please cross the road and go down a narrow path opposite. At the end, turn right and follow the lane to the end. Where it bears right, turn left and up a steep hill to Clayhill Farm into the bridlepath. This is a bit boggy in places, and at the time of writing, clear. If in doubt, phone BHS Bridleways Officer, Mrs Rigby (0787 310217). At the end of Clay Lane, bear left for a short distance then right into a cart track, over a crossroads and on to Hitcham for further refreshment at the local; or turn right by Swifts Manor and finish at Monks Eleigh.

19 The Peddar's Way

Approx. 112k, 70 miles

OS maps 144, 143, 132

Start: 912883:OS 144

Finish: 708431:OS 132

There is much dispute about the origins of the Peddar's Way, with some contending that it was built by the Romans to bring soldiers between Lincolnshire and the heart of East Anglia, using a ferry crossing over the Wash at Heacham. (To support this theory are the uprisings that took place around the same time; Boudicaans were attacking various Roman settlements, including Colchester.) The route would have run from the Wash (where it still exists) to Colchester (where it doesn't). Others suggest that the way is much older and pre-dates the Romans: barrows lining its route reinforce this theory.

Now the route peters out just north-east of Thetford (south of the A11), though there are plans to extend it further south, if the various rivers can be crossed.

The original Peddar's Way (from the Latin 'ped' meaning foot, presumably because of the numbers of foot travellers) was an engineering feat, with huge embankments and a width of 45 feet. Typical of Roman roads, it is very straight, though the horse route diverts from the straight path, because many of the rights of way have been lost. Even now, the excellence of the construction of the way can be seen: I rode it in the wettest spring for years, and yet it was not poached or muddy, and the grassy track was a delight to ride.

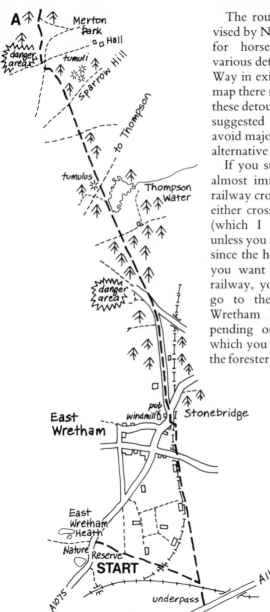

The route below has been devised by Norfolk County Council for horse riders, and makes various detours from the Peddar's Way in existence. Though on the map there may seem no reason for these detours, believe me, they are suggested with good reason – to avoid major roads, and to provide alternative bridlepaths.

If you start from the A11 you almost immediately encounter a railway crossing, which you must either cross or use the underpass (which I wouldn't recommend unless you are on a Shetland pony, since the height is only 5 feet). If you want to start north of the railway, you take the A1076 and go to the north end of East Wretham Nature Reserve. Depending on the direction from which you approach, you will see the forester's house (913883) either

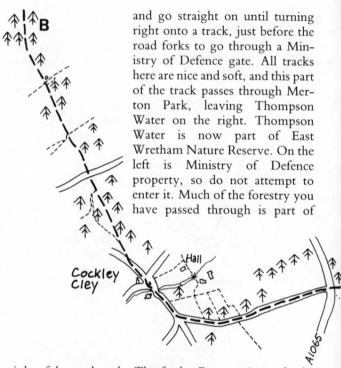

and go straight on until turning right onto a track, just before the road forks to go through a Ministry of Defence gate. All tracks here are nice and soft, and this part of the track passes through Merton Park, leaving Thompson Water on the right. Thompson Water is now part of East Wretham Nature Reserve. On the left is Ministry of Defence property, so do not attempt to enter it. Much of the forestry you have passed through is part of

on the left or right of the road, and opposite this a track leading to the way. If you want to take your box down the end and park, you must ring the warden (Forestry Commission: 095 382 235) to get the barrier taken down. You go to the end of this track, almost to the railway crossing, then turn left onto the Peddar's Way proper. Cross a minor road, and continue till the next road, near the Stonebridge Windmill (built about 1875) where you turn right onto the road, and pass some shops and a post office. At the sign of the Peddar's Way to the left, turn left,

Thetford Forest (owned by Forestry Commission) which is now the largest forest of its kind in lowland Britain; much of the land was previously heathland.

Follow the tracks, crossing the road Sparrow Hill, and going through Merton Park (the park is mainly on your right, and in the distance you can see Merton Hall). Merton Hall, which dates back to the 17th century, was the site of the original true life version of *Babes in the Wood*: the wicked uncle lived here and he is supposed to have tried to lure the children to their deaths in Wayland Wood where they reputedly still wail.

Just north of Home Farm is a crossing of tracks (903992) where you turn left and continue till you meet the main B1108. Turn left along this road, which is probably the worst bit of roadwork in the entire route. It is a busy road, so take care. Turn right off the main road into Little Cressingham, and opposite the pub turn right.

Follow this minor road to the B1077, turning briefly left onto this road (862044) to South Pickenham. Just before you reach Pickenham Hall on the left, you cross the River Wissey, where you can water your horse. (Access beside road bridge.) Pickenham Hall was built in 1903 to replace an earlier 18th-century house. Gatehouse beside the church. The house is open to the public and they serve teas.

Just beside the church, go left off the road, and follow a minor road until a T junction, where you go straight ahead on a rough track. This pleasant soft track leads to the A1065; straight over and follow this long straight road with wide grassy verges to Cockley Cley, turning right onto the minor road just before Cockley Cley. On the left is the Iceni Village, which was built in 1971 and represents a Boudicaan type settlement of about AD 61. There are traces of a moat and well, suggesting that there was a settlement there. On

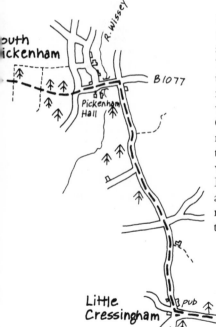

the other side of the road is the museum. Cockley Cley park and hall can be seen on the right. In Cockley Cley village, take the middle turning, in front of you, leaving the church on your left. Carry on up this road, until you meet a public bridleway on the right, which you follow. Shortly after this pleasant, soft track begins, it forks. The right hand fork is marked with ominous signs about firing. If there is firing in progress then you must divert to the left and skirt the wood, which is actually a better surface for riding anyway. If they are not firing you may ride through the wood, and follow the old Icknield Way (leading from Hunstanton to Avebury in Wiltshire).

The two tracks meet up before the next road, which you cross; and (map 143) the next; then, follow the track to the end of the wood, where you turn right and join the old Fincham Drove (an old Roman Road between Smallburgh in Broadland and Denver on the edge of the Fens – map 132). Over the A47 (778104) taking care, as this is a fast, busy road; follow straight ahead without being diverted to the left, tempting though this may look. The track here is in danger of being ploughed up and cropped, but its

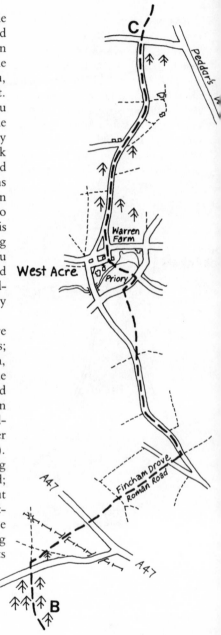

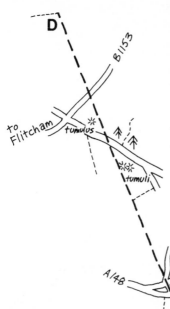

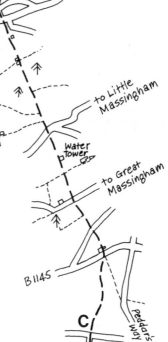

ford and keep straight on past the sign of the Stag Inn (a small inn on the left of the road which you might easily miss). Straight over the next road junction (787152) and right at the next. Follow this road for about 3 miles to the T junction, then straight on along a track till the route turns into the Peddar's Way proper (792210).

This next 10 miles is the best riding in the entire route: rolling countryside with hardly a house in sight, and a broad, soft track stretching ahead of you. The track route continues straight ahead until the next road, which you cross, and on to the next, where you turn left (797117). Follow this road to the top of the hill over-looking the delightful village of West Acre (where there are re-mains of an Augustinian Priory founded 1150 – it is not open to the public). As the road is about to descend into West Acre, turn right on to a track (788138) then, after about 30 yards turn left, beside a hedge. Keep by the hedge, going downhill, and at the barn keep straight along a track until the next road. Turn right and follow the road till the ford sign, then turn left along a sandy track across West Acre Common. Cross the

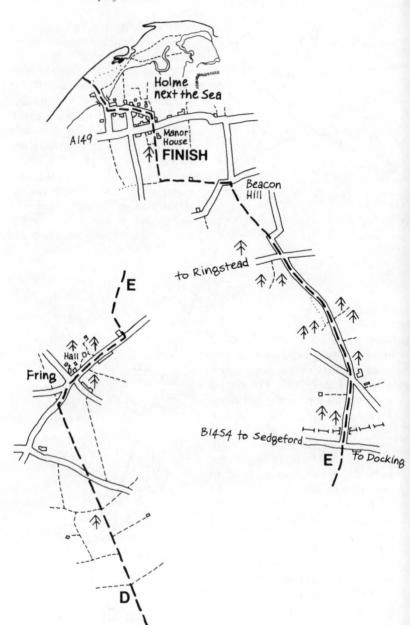

Holme next the Sea

A149

Manor House

FINISH

Beacon Hill

to Ringstead

E

Hall

Fring

B1454 to Sedgeford

E

To Docking

D

crosses several roads, but just carry on until you arrive at a metal road, where you turn right into the village of Fring. Continue on this road, in Fring, straight ahead, ignoring right hand turnings, and then, some way out of the village, turn left on to a track just past a barn. Follow this to the next road (748372). Here you will see the old Docking workhouse on the right. Straight over this road and the next two roads. Then, when the road bends to the right, continue uphill along a bridleway. At the top is a triangulation point for the summit of Beacon Hill and the sea can be seen. At the next road turn

briefly left and then take the track leading to the right. This leads you along parallel to the shore, above Thornham and Holme. Before reaching the windmill, turn right onto a stony path (a deep gulley to the left) which will bring you out on to the A149 in Holme. This is where the route ends. If you want to sample the delights of the beach (a huge expanse of sand) then follow the road straight ahead and continue round to the left, passing through the village till you come to a T junction, where you turn right. Go through the golf course and you will find yourself on the beach.

An excellent leaflet on this route is available from Planning Dept, Norfolk County Council, Martineau Lane, Norwich NR1 2DH
Tel: (0603) 611122

Local contacts:

Mrs Cleasby-Thompson,
Blackhill House, The Arms,
Little Cressingham, Norfolk
Tel: (0953) 882465

Forestry Commission Office,
Bridgham, East Wretham
Tel: (095 382) 235

Mr & Mrs C. Boone,
The Warren, West Acre,
Norfolk
Tel: (076 05) 251

Miss Bannister,
Home Farm, West Acre High House,
Castle Acre, Norfolk
Tel: (076 05) 342

Forestry Commission District Office for Thetford Forest and Norfolk:
Santon Downham, Brandon,
Suffolk
Tel: Thetford 810271

20 The Weavers' Way

Approx. 24k, 15 miles

OS map 133

Start: 186277:OS 133

Finish: 368253:OS 133

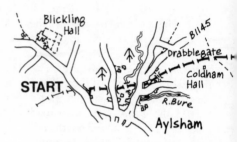

Another disused railway line which has been opened to walkers and riders; called the Weavers' Way because of the significance of the weaving industry in this part of East Anglia, the way passes through some pleasant countryside and starts near historic Blick-

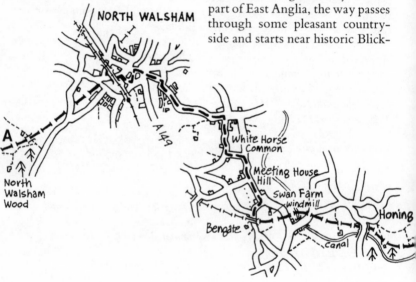

ling, with the National Trust Blickling Hall. As with all disused railway lines, there is a problem of access: do not assume that because the line crosses a road that you can reach it from that road – because it

Aylsham (Drabblegate), so you must turn left onto the former Aylsham to North Walsham road and follow it for about half a mile. Turn right onto a green lane, cross the bypass and continue along the green lane to a former level crossing house. Turn left, rejoining railway line.

In North Walsham, walk through town centre, past Market Cross and 14th-century church, take road signposted to Bengate. Almost out of the town turn left into Thirlby Road, keeping straight on at the end of the road along the footpath across the field. Left onto minor road, right at next junction and right again into Holgate Lane. Then first left and next right, and follow the road to Bengate. Just before the bypass turn left onto the disused railway line once more.

A diversion is necessary in the route from Bengate to Stalham – follow diversion signs. Turn right by The Gate House (which was a level crossing house) and cross the canal. Turn right back onto disused railway line by former Honing Station.

As with all disused railway lines, this one is not a right of way but a permissive path, and you are requested to bear in mind walkers who may be using it.

A leaflet on the Weavers' Way is available from Norfolk County Council.

may be in a tunnel or on a bridge. Car parks with access are available at Felmingham Station, North Walsham and Bengate as well as at each end, Stalham and Blickling Hall (which is by courtesy of the National Trust: you are requested to make a contribution to its upkeep).

The route is easy enough to follow and offers some opportunities for a canter, although some parts are still composed of the clinker from the original line which is not good for horses. If starting at Blickling, be careful not to miss the entrance, which is under a bridge and very small. The railway line temporarily stops at

21   A Pennine Way Route for Horses

with help of Mrs Boon

Approx. 324k, 202 miles

OS maps 109, 103, 104, 98, 91

Start: 977020:OS 109

Finish: 931189:OS 91

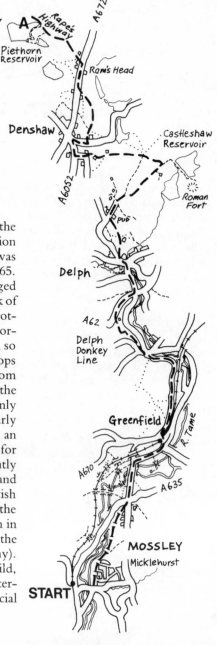

The Pennine Way is one of the longest Countryside Commission long distance footpaths, and was the first to be completed in 1965. It runs through wild, rugged countryside, starting in the Peak of Derbyshire and ending at the Scottish border. The hills and moorland are treacherous and boggy, so beware, particularly on the flat tops of the hills, and do not stray from the given path. Unfortunately the long distance path is footpath only for much of its length, particularly the southern end, but this is an alternative route devised for horses, commencing slightly further north, at Mossley, and stopping short of the Scottish border. The Pennine Way was the suggestion of Tom Stephenson in 1935, and he has written the official guide (see Bibliography). This route crosses some wild, beautiful and still dangerous terrain; much of it follows the official Pennine Way.

Mossley – Todmorden
22k, 14 miles
Warland – Moor Side
24k, 15 miles

Start at the disused railway line at Mossley, which has been converted to recreational use, with a good grit surface. Cross A635 and rejoin the railway line till meeting minor road at Greenfield, where there is parking space. Turn left and follow minor road to the A669, turning left and crossing the river; a quick left and right over the railway bring you to a track marked 'Saddleworth Golf Club' going right uphill; take this track, which is tarmaced but not busy, and wind up hill, going under disused railway to rejoin the A6052. Left onto this road, and left again brings you to the Delph Donkey Line; follow this briefly under two bridges; then you must escape to the right through one of the gaps in the wall and join the road that runs parallel. Continue uphill along this track till it brings you out on the A62, which you cross; straight over on another track, leading through a farmyard and bringing you to a minor road; bearing right, you arrive in Delph.

Here you must use the main road through the village, and after left-hand bend, take turning to right marked cul-de-sac. The metal road turns into bridleway coming through the fields and arrives at a minor road by a pub

and disused church. Turn right and follow the road straight on; it becomes a rough track traversing the moor and dipping to Castleshaw Reservoir. On the opposite side of the reservoir can be seen the remains of a Roman Fort. At the reservoir, take the left track and follow it till it brings you to the A6052; right into Denshaw and first right, past the houses on the left until what appears to be a drive, leading into a farmyard, but which is a bridleway, slightly kinked to the right, bisected by a footpath. This bridleway runs between the characteristic dry stone walls, but, despite local protests, may be blocked by heavy iron bedsteads doing duty as gates, but totally immovable. Having negotiated this, emerge by stone houses onto A672 (977116) (waymarked bridleway) and follow right till Ram's Head pub on the left, after which take waymarked bridleway through stone walls (again, there may be problems here with the farmer sheep dipping) and onto a wide expanse of moor, traversed by an ancient track known as the Rape's Highway; the moors either side of the track are inviting, but do beware of bogs. The track becomes rough and steep leading down to Piethorn Reservoir; where tracks diverge, fork left, then soon right and left.

When water pumping station is on your right, go through the gate

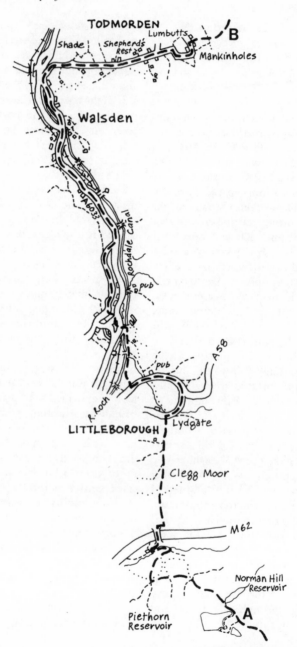

TODMORDEN
Lumbutts
Shade
Shepherds
Rest
pln
Mankinholes
B

Walsden

A6033

Rochdale Canal

pub

pub
A58

R. Roch

LITTLEBOROUGH
Lydgate

Clegg Moor

M62

Norman Hill
Reservoir

Piethorn
Reservoir
A

and uphill to cross the M62 by bridge. Turn right down a stony track and cross Clegg Moor. Follow bridleway to minor road at Lydgate, where turn right to main A58, where you turn left. Pass several turnings to the right and take that marked Lightowlers Lane, a rough track leading past houses, forking left down towards the canal; keep on the east side of the canal and go past Fothergill and Harvey works (where track becomes metalled) and over the bridge onto main road. Left onto A58 and immediately right up bridleway over a minor road and into a small narrow bridleway, finishing at minor road (945185).

You are now onto map 103. This empty, gently descending road is preferable to the main road, which, unfortunately you must join before Walsden. Good grass verges however. Having crossed the river, fork right to Lumbutts up minor road, going through Shade, past the Shepherd's Rest pub and in Lumbutts doing 2 sides of a square (right and then left) then take bridleway to the left, which leads towards the hospital. Although the bridleway continues along the side of the hill, it is not advisable due to bogs, and we suggest that you take the road beside the hospital, turn right down cul-de-sac and before the next hospital take a right-hand track; the cattle grid has a bridle gate, and follow this rough track

uphill, forking left to join an old packhorse route, London Road, which runs behind a drystone wall along the bottom of the hill. Stoodley Pike, a 120-ft obelisk, is above you on the top of the hill, commemorating the Battle of Waterloo. London Road will then descend steeply into Charlestown. Past Erringden Grange, turn left onto minor road which will take you over Rochdale Canal and into Hebden Bridge. Here are alternative routes: either a long stretch of roadwork, but avoid the main road, and detour to the delightful village of Heptonstall, or take the much shorter route through Hebden Bridge on the main road.

Alternative detour: take minor road from centre of Hebden Bridge (987272) and call in at Heptonstall. This stone village is set high in the hills overlooking Hardcastle Crags and the wooded valley. Once a weaving community, the village clusters round narrow cobbled streets, and boasts the oldest Methodist chapel in the world (built 1764): a delightful octagonal building with first-floor balcony; the two churches are also interesting: particularly the ruined one, possibly built in 1260, which was damaged in a storm in 1847 and left as a ruin; it had two aisles, and the ruin is more attractive than the Victorian new church the other side of the graveyard.

The houses of Heptonstall and

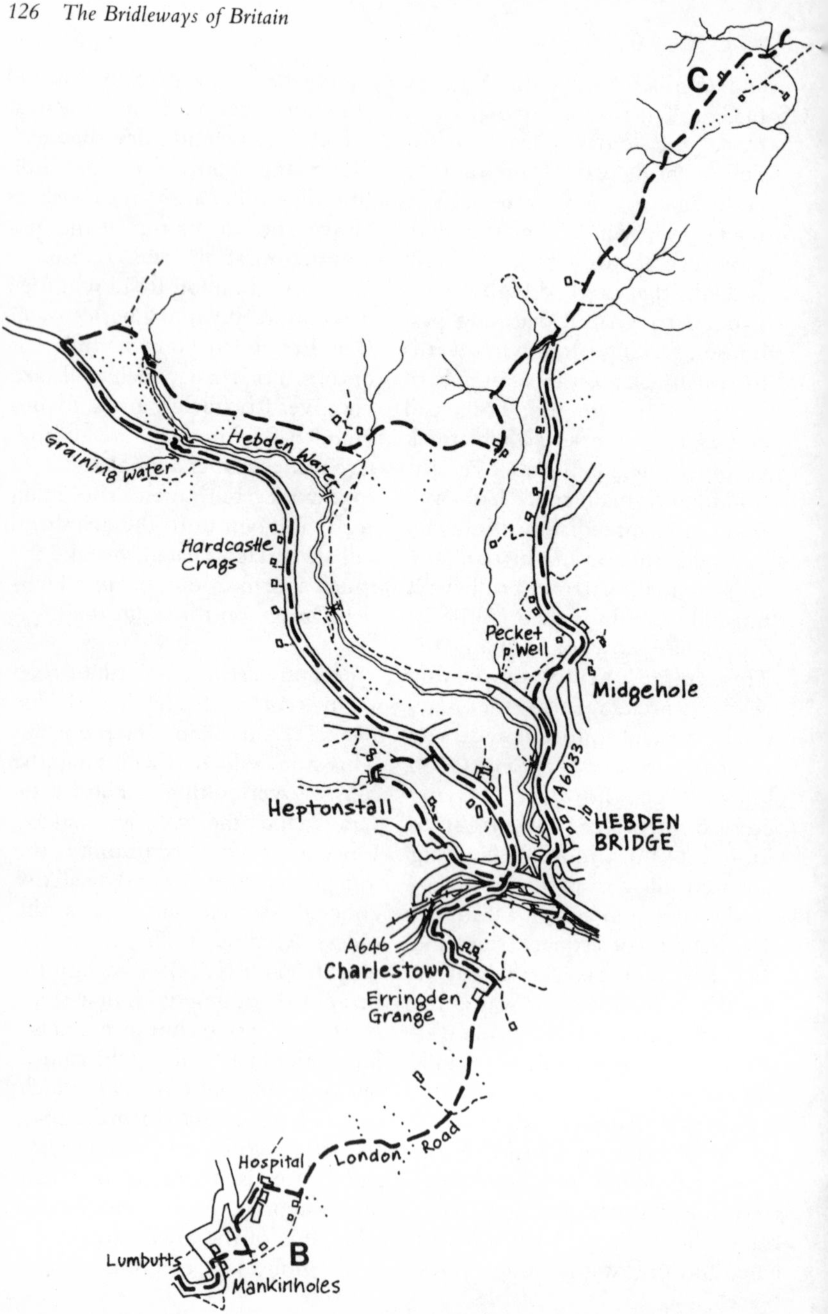
C
Graining Water
Hebden Water
Hardcastle Crags
Pecket Well
Midgehole
A6033
Heptonstall
HEBDEN BRIDGE
A646
Charlestown
Erringden Grange
London Road
Hospital
Lumbutts
B
Mankinholes

Hebden Bridge are remarkable, built of huge blocks of stone and, particularly in the town, many storeys high; some houses rise up the hillside in such a way that the front door one side is on a different floor from the front door the other side.

If taking the detour, follow minor road for some 3 miles till you cross Graining Water, take a few hairpin bends and eventually find the official Pennine Way leading through white gates off to the right. You will divert again to the south-east and follow Hebden Water striking off on the bridle-way across the hill (973314) and joining minor road.

Main route: tolerating main roads and centre of Hebden Bridge: arrive in main street (A6033), turn right then left and fork left down minor road to Midgehole (993281); after half a mile, take waymarked bridleway on right, which leads to Pecket Well and the main A6033. Another stretch of main road until minor road to the left (993304) which bears north-easterly, turning into a track and arriving at Moor Side and onto OS map 104. This is an unmaintained public road.

Moor Side – East Marton
32k, 20 miles
East Marton – Helwith Bridge
38k, 24 miles
Helwith Bridge – Hawes
29k, 18 miles
Hawes – E. Mellwaters
48k, 30 miles

At Moor Side turn left and follow road until second turning on right to Haworth. Haworth is worth a visit if only for its associations with the Brontës; the town is small and compact, high on a hill, with of course many tourist shops and the old parsonage where the Brontës lived, which has been turned into a small museum, with relics of the sisters, manuscripts and paintings by Branwell. Take the minor road going north towards Lane End and follow through to White Hill and Lane Ends (979438). (Back to OS map 103.)

At the A6068 go right and then immediately left, over crossroads, forking right and at T junction turning left. At the next crossroads turn left towards Dale End and Lothersdale. Before you enter Dale End (past the church) there is a parking place and bridlepath is signposted going north. This is a good broad track which meets a hard track, and you turn left down this hard surface until the track becomes bridleway again through walls, and up to join a minor road where you must go through a

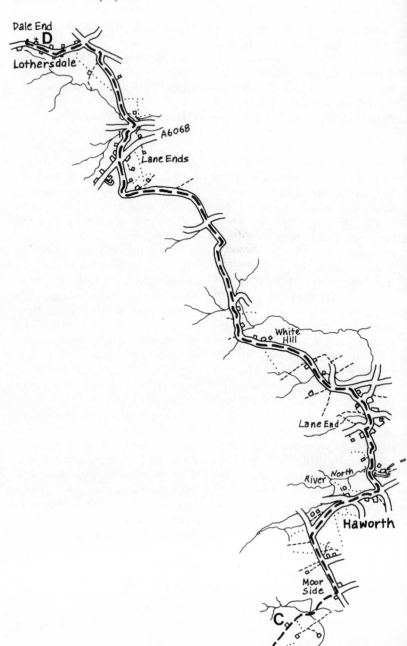

gate. Right along minor road and left at T junction; straight over crossroads going down a walled road, drystone walls, high on the moors and on to Elslack, where a right and a left over the A56 bring you out onto the A59 which you must follow for about half a mile through East Marton. At 905510 a track with broad entrance leads through fields, alternatively stony and muddy but well marked, passing Ingthorpe Grange on left and onto a metal surface to join minor road, where you turn right.

The next left turn leads to another old track on the right (884530) which is based on stone, but becomes pretty muddy; this passes right in front of beautiful stone Stainton Cotes house and turns into a metal road flanked with new houses and onto the A65. Right and left here at Coniston Cold and the road will take you under the railway. Left at the crossroads, signposted to Bell Busk, and just before Haven Flatt, where bed and breakfast is offered, turn right down waymarked bridleway going through various gates, and over a stone bridge. This bridleway is well signposted with blue paint marks on walls and gate posts, and you are asked to follow the fence to the left of the first field. Some good turf here, though there is livestock about. The track winds between drystone walls through a farmyard and past Kirk Syke, where the track is

metalled, and finally to Airton, where you turn right onto the minor road (904588) going north (onto map 98).

Through Kirkby Malham and Malham, in the Yorkshire Dales National Park, and onto crossroads (905656). Turn left, following signs to Malham Tarn, which is National Trust and a wildlife sanctuary. Just before the tarn, a beautiful lake, surrounded by hills, go through the car park and follow the green track, a bridleway, winding around the perimeter of the lake. Keep the wood on your left and rejoin the stone track. The track is a bridleway and will take you round the lake, behind Malham Tarn Field Centre and out to Water Houses where you rejoin the minor road, turning left, forking right and right again and continuing along this road for about 4 miles till Sannat Hall Farm (834687). At the T junction turn left and immediately right down a country road leading to Helwith Bridge, taking the left at the T junction of paths. At Helwith Bridge you must join the B6479 going north (right) to Horton in Ribblesdale.

Here, just before crossing the river, take the minor road marked cul-de-sac going north. This road leads between stone walls for about 4 miles to High Birkwith Farm. Go through the yard and follow the track, which is an old packhorse route, bearing right

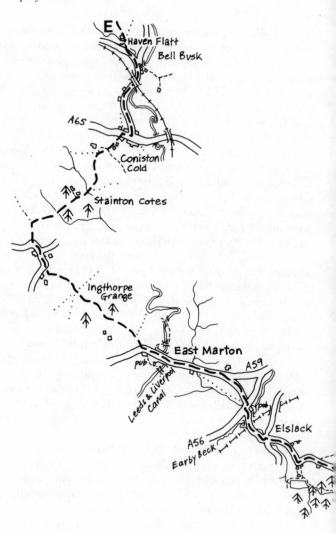

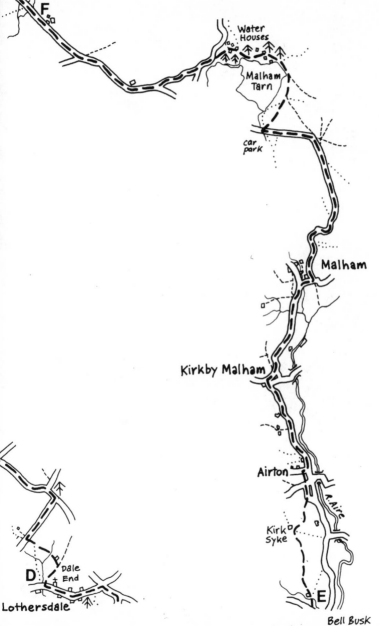

F

Water
Houses

Malham
Tarn

car
park

Malham

Kirkby Malham

Airton

R. Aire

Kirk
Syke

D

Dale
End

Lothersdale

E

Bell Busk

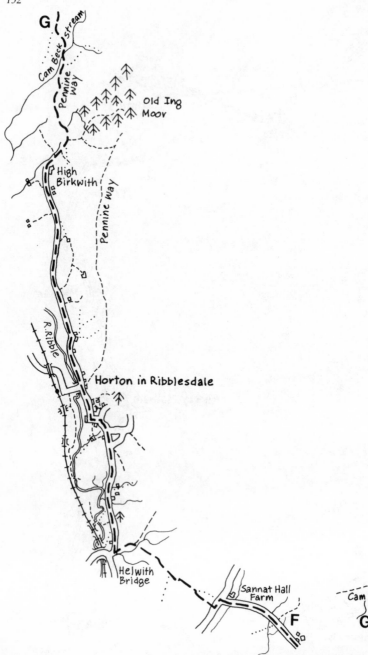

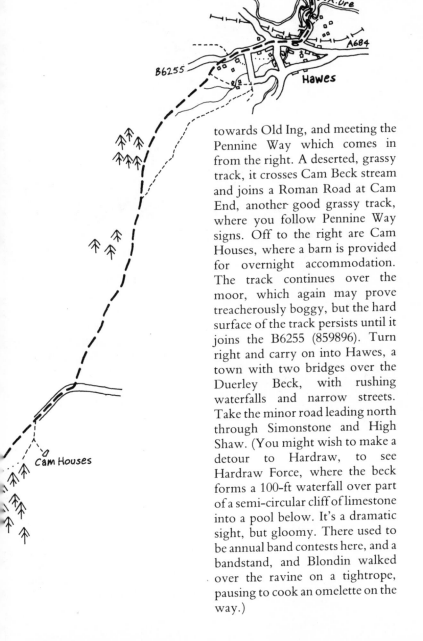

towards Old Ing, and meeting the Pennine Way which comes in from the right. A deserted, grassy track, it crosses Cam Beck stream and joins a Roman Road at Cam End, another good grassy track, where you follow Pennine Way signs. Off to the right are Cam Houses, where a barn is provided for overnight accommodation. The track continues over the moor, which again may prove treacherously boggy, but the hard surface of the track persists until it joins the B6255 (859896). Turn right and carry on into Hawes, a town with two bridges over the Duerley Beck, with rushing waterfalls and narrow streets. Take the minor road leading north through Simonstone and High Shaw. (You might wish to make a detour to Hardraw, to see Hardraw Force, where the beck forms a 100-ft waterfall over part of a semi-circular cliff of limestone into a pool below. It's a dramatic sight, but gloomy. There used to be annual band contests here, and a bandstand, and Blondin walked over the ravine on a tightrope, pausing to cook an omelette on the way.)

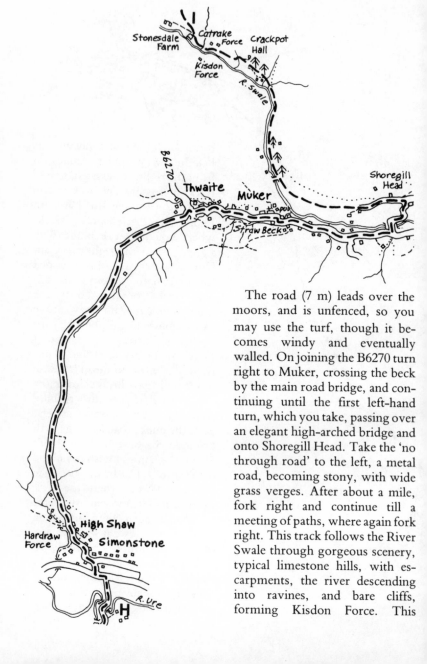

The road (7 m) leads over the moors, and is unfenced, so you may use the turf, though it becomes windy and eventually walled. On joining the B6270 turn right to Muker, crossing the beck by the main road bridge, and continuing until the first left-hand turn, which you take, passing over an elegant high-arched bridge and onto Shoregill Head. Take the 'no through road' to the left, a metal road, becoming stony, with wide grass verges. After about a mile, fork right and continue till a meeting of paths, where again fork right. This track follows the River Swale through gorgeous scenery, typical limestone hills, with escarpments, the river descending into ravines, and bare cliffs, forming Kisdon Force. This makes a beautiful ride, though the track itself is stony and your pace will be limited (OS map 91). The track crosses Catrake Force, a waterfall with huge flags above and below, where there is a wooden bridge. The track will bring you through Stonesdale Farm and climbs on uphill signposted Pennine Way. The surface becomes softer and there are good opportunities for a gallop, though do beware of sudden streams and

boggy patches. Magnificent views of rolling hills, dotted with typical drystone barns, one in almost every field, used for cattle and hay, and crisscrossed with drystone walls. Through a farmyard, and then, when the route becomes less well defined, follow the cairns. These will guide you to the best crossings of streams, etc. Towards Tan Hill the surface improves, with another possibility of a gallop. At Tan Hill is a desolate pub where you might find refreshment, but we found only a desolate horse tethered outside and the pub closed.

Turn right here and follow the metal road to the fork (899075). Turn left and follow rough track. This track winds over a moor which, apart from the odd stream,

offers heathery, rough grass, good
riding, and splendid views. The
road becomes tarmaced again at
Sleightholme, and there should be
a bridleway leading over the hill to
God's Bridge here. However,
when we went the gates were
wired up, and the only detour
would be via Trough Heads. Here
you can stay b & b in an isolated
stone house high on the moor;
have a special all day breakfast for
£2, or an evening meal 'guaranteed
no chips' for £2. Home-made
bread. If calling in at Trough
Heads you can join the bridleway
at the back of the house and follow
telegraph poles down hill to join a
track (964126) going east into East
Mellwaters. A detour to God's
Bridge is advised, though you
may again have problems with
bridleways blocked by wired-up
gates. The bridge is a natural stone
bridge over the River Greta, with
springs and gulleys and huge stone
slabs. The track will bring you out
eventually on the A66, a very busy
road with horrible fast moving
traffic, which you must follow
(turn left) for about a mile.

East Mellwaters – Baldersdale
10k, 6 miles

Just past the farmhouse at 956129
you will see the sign on the right
for the Pennine Way (it is bridleway here) which takes you
through a gate which has been
massively barricaded with binder
twine and wire. (Wire cutters may
be necessary.) The path rises over
the moors, and is erratically
marked with cairns; do not stray
from the path because the land is
extremely boggy. You will cross
several streams, the second one of
which has a footbridge too narrow
for horses, but the stream is
certainly fordable. Just after this
the Pennine Way uses a stile
(although it is a bridleway) so you
may have to divert through the
wall to your right using a gate, and
then return past the stile through
the next gate to your left. Apart
from dampness, the path is good
and grassy and you should make
good speed until you reach the
road at Baldersdale; here you must
turn left again until the farmyard,
when you turn left again just
before the farm buildings onto a
hard road, which takes you up
between the reservoirs (through a
gate) and out onto the minor road
(931189).

This is the end of the route that I
would advise. There is plenty of
space near the reservoir for parking and loading and unloading of
boxes.

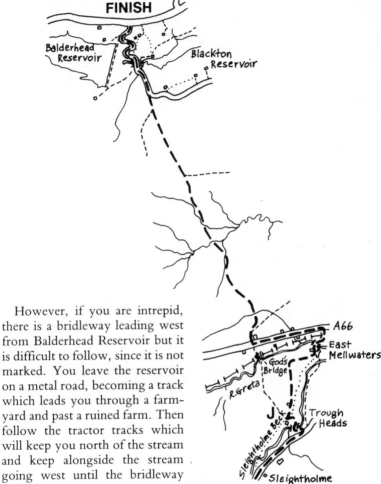

FINISH

Balderhead Reservoir

Blackton Reservoir

A66

East Mellwaters

Gods Bridge

R.Greta

J

Trough Heads

Sleightholme Bec

Sleightholme

However, if you are intrepid, there is a bridleway leading west from Balderhead Reservoir but it is difficult to follow, since it is not marked. You leave the reservoir on a metal road, becoming a track which leads you through a farm-yard and past a ruined farm. Then follow the tractor tracks which will keep you north of the stream and keep alongside the stream going west until the bridleway makes a curious excursion across the stream at the point where several streams meet, and then re-crosses the Balder Beck a little further on. The going becomes more and more boggy and the landscape more and more desolate but eventually if you follow the stream till 848164 you will cross the stream just before its source and meet up with a wide, walled track leading you towards the minor road to North Stainmore. (Approx. 14k, 9 miles)

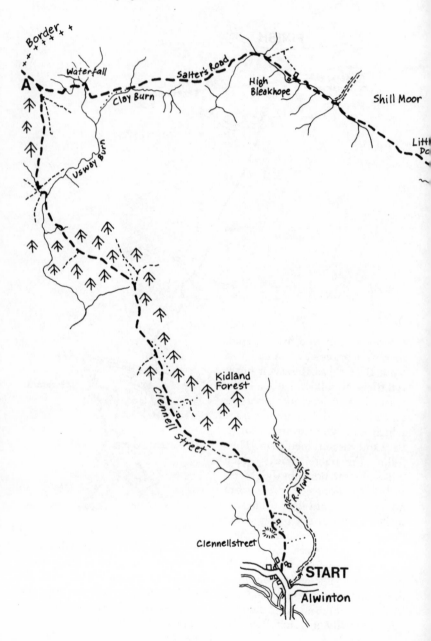

Border

Waterfall

Salter's Road

Cloy Burn

High Bleakhope

Shill Moor

Uswhy Burn

Littl
Do

Kidland
Forest

Clennell street

R. Alwin

Clennellstreet

START

Alwinton

22 Clennell Street and Salter's Road

suggested by Margery Price

Approx. 46k, 29 miles

OS maps 80, 81

Start: 922064:OS 80

Finish: 990110:OS 81

Clennell Street is recommended as a beautiful ride in splendid scenery, Salter's Road is extremely badly marked so only embark on the round trip if your map reading is excellent.

Clennell Street

Falling within the Northumberland National Park, the Clennell Street old Roman Road is well marked at its southern end, and the surface is a good, flinty one. The path soon opens out into grassy moorland, and becomes softer. The scenery is rolling, with views either side, and the track leads invitingly on to the Scottish border. There are a few gates but they don't present any problems, and a few slightly boggy patches, but nothing to worry about. The route leads through Forestry Commission (Kidland Forest), where you fork left to follow the better marked track. Meet a hard surfaced road and cross it going uphill towards the border. Again,

this is a delightful track, soft and springy and with splendid views. You can carry on over the border to Cocklawfoot, but if you wish to make the round trip, using the Salter's Road, you must take the second bridle gate to your right (875157) which is not marked in any way.

Salter's Road was an old drove road used to transport salt. It leads you by means of a much narrower path through a new forestry plantation. There is no problem here in following the track – if in doubt, use the wooden posts that define the path. You cross various forestry tracks, and Usway Burn just above the small waterfall. Follow the Clay Burn, and when meeting a hard surfaced forestry road, join it briefly before following the small green stakes off it again to the north. Your problems begin when you leave Forestry Commission land, and the path is very badly marked; you should arrive in two small paddocks, go through them onto a metalled road by a farmhouse (keeping the stream in general to your right). The metalled road takes you to another farmhouse in this valley, then turns off northeast whilst your bridleway is a well marked flinty track taking you up to the ridge ahead. Unfortunately on the top of the ridge the path again becomes obscure and the going (in winter) a bit boggy (OS map 81). You will also have to ford several streams. You are now going south-east, crossing Little Dod (keep near the fence as the slopes are very steep) and over Shank Burn. The landscape here is wild but beautiful in a bleak way.

Shank House is marked on the map and should be a landmark, but it is hidden behind a new forestry plantation; so head for that. After some problems with finding the bridleway after this, we opted to take the road back to Alnham here (964134) but you could be adventurous and set off over the next two hills on the true Salter's Road which comes out by the church at Alnham. There are in this area many old settlements of interest; note also Alnham Pele Tower (beside the church). These medieval local strongholds where people could safely keep their livestock in times of raiding over the border are a local feature.

To get back to the beginning of the Clennell Street drove road, you must take the yellow minor road through Biddlestone, Rookland and back to Clennell.

23 Salter Fell Drove Road

suggested by Margery Price

Approx. 16k, 10 miles

OS maps 97, 103

Start: 607625:OS 97
Finish: 697544:OS 103

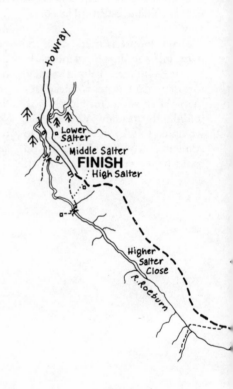

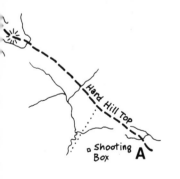

An old drove road that winds over the moors from High Salter to Slaidburn; magnificent views in remote countryside with not a house to be seen. Approach from the north up metal road as far as farm at High Salter and follow the track through a couple of gates. Sign at entrance 'No through road to Slaidburn'. The track is stony (sharp stones, too) all the way, so don't expect to gallop it. The moors either side of the track vary: sometimes being boggy, and other times springy turf, and later heather.

24 The Hambleton Drove Road

suggested by Margery Price

Approx. 25k, 15 miles

OS map 100

Start: 556772:OS 100

Finish: 471994:OS 100

The Hambleton Drove Road was part of an ancient highway, originally a 'ridgeway' running from the south of England to Scotland. Although some of it has been tarmaced, this section remains as a track over the moors. The drovers' roads were favoured by drovers as an alternative to the turnpikes which were too expensive for them. This stretch, parts of which are green lane and parts of which are bridleway, forms a section of the Cleveland Way walking route.

Start at the southern end, near which was the Hambleton Race Ground, where racing took place from about 1613 to 1776. Racing stables still exist near here and gallops cross the way. A large stone opposite Dialstone House is supposed to have been the position of the weighing machine and the name of the house is said to be derived from the dial or weighing machine. Further up the old road you pass various quarries, relics of the lime industry; also several

barrows and earthworks.

Later you pass one of the oldest inns on the route – Chequers – which is now a farm, but which will serve soft drinks to travellers. On the wall is the old inn sign, a chequer board with the following inscription below:

Be not in haste: Step in and taste; Good ale for nothing – tomorrow

An excellent leaflet is available on this route from The North York Moors National Park Information Service, The Old Vicarage, Helmsley, North Yorks, YO6 5BP Tel: (04392) 657

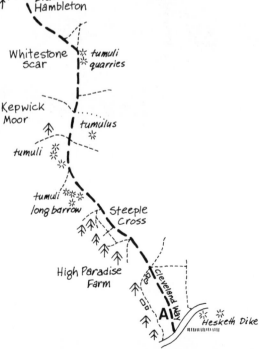

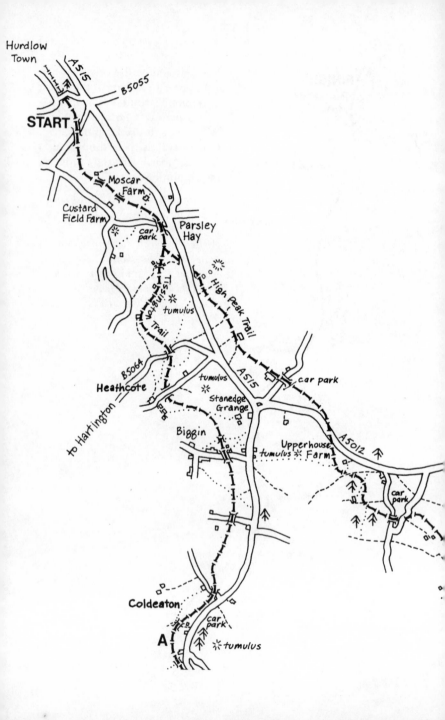

25 The High Peak and Tissington Trails

recommended by Mrs R.C. Eld

Tissington Trail

Approx. 20k, 13 miles

OS map 119

Start: 176469:OS 119
Finish: 147633:OS 119

High Peak Trail

Approx. 28k, 17½ miles

OS map 119

Start: 312560:OS 119
Finish: 124667:OS 119

Many councils have taken an enlightened line on disused railways and provided walking and riding routes on them (though some councils make such severe restrictions on riders – only allowing them to walk – that their routes are really useless. This is why I have not included in the book the Durham railway walks which cover a large area near Durham.) These railway routes are not rights of way, but permissive paths, and the permission of the council must be sought for sponsored rides, etc. The surface is good going, mostly

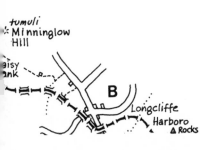

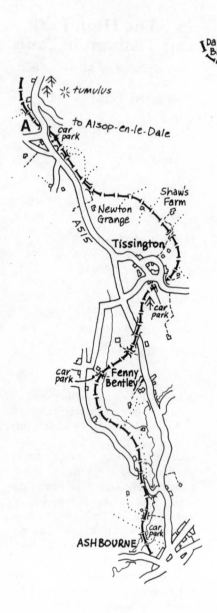

tumulus

A

car park

to Alsop-en-le-Dale

Shaw's Farm

Newton Grange

A515

Tissington

car park

car park

Fenny Bentley

car park

ASHBOURNE

Daisy Bank

Longcliffe

B

Harboro Rocks

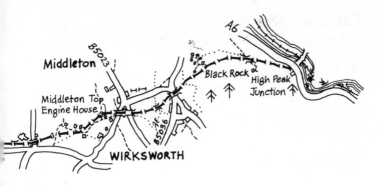

canterable, and there are several parking spots: Mapleton Lane, Ashbourne, Tissington, Alsop-en-le-Bale, Hartington (recommended), Parsley Hay, Hurdlow, Friden, Minninglow and Thorpe; Black Rocks, Middleton Top Engine House. Water for horses available at Mapleton Lane, Hartington.

Don't forget that access to railway lines is not always easy – these car parks all provide access. Also, please remember there may be walkers on the path just ahead of you who won't appreciate being mown down by galloping horses. Otherwise, enjoy the good route with splendid countryside and interesting railway history.

An excellent series of leaflets produced by the Derbyshire County Planning Department and the Peak Park Office, the Peak Park Office, Baslow Road, Bakewell, Derbyshire DE4 1AE Tel: (062 981) 2881

26 Circular Route near Hythe

Mrs S.W. Ashenden-Bax

Approx. 40k, 25 miles

OS map 189

Start and finish: 120350:OS189

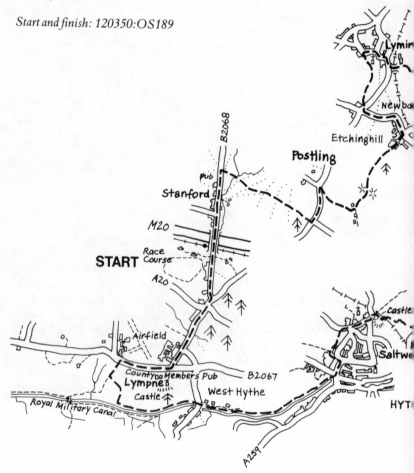

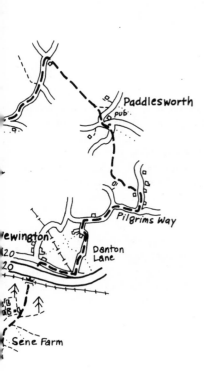

This route was used as the East Kent Golden Horseshoe Qualifier, which had the racecourse as a starting point. But since the route is circular, you could start anywhere on it. If commencing at the racecourse, turn right onto road, continue straight until the A20, where you turn right and then take second road on left to Lympne. At T junction with B2067 turn right; continue for about half a mile, passing County Members pub on the left and the airfield on the right. Opposite the main airport entrance, turn left onto bridleway. Follow hard track downhill onto mud track and through open gate. Turn left at the bottom of the wood, following Wildlife Park boundary. Keep boundary chain link fence on your right. At the bottom of the hill, cross over wooden bridge.

Turn left along muddy track. But *please note* that this is not a public bridleway and permission to use this section must be sought from John Aspinal, Fort Lympne Wildlife Park. Carry straight on for a couple of miles, taking the track on the left of the grass bank. (But don't go on grass bank, please.) Cross straight over road, and the track continues and goes into Green Lane. At the end of Green Lane turn left onto the main road and shortly turn right up the steep hill – Barrack Hill. At the top of the hill, turn left, signposted 'Saltwood'. At right-hand bend in road, turn left down the track in front of white house called Pine Trees (154351).

At the end of the close-boarded fence, turn right and follow track at the back of the houses, turning right and continuing in a straight line on the track between rear gardens and school playing field for a short distance. Keep to the right at the fork in tracks and beware people, bicycles and prams. Turn right at the road and after about 50 yards turn left beside the War Memorial and continue down Grange Road.

At the T junction turn left down 'No Through Road'. Right into Saltwood Castle grounds through black iron bridleway gate, by bridleway signpost. Follow the track, keeping iron fence on your right, and take second bridleway on left and proceed under brick tunnel, through green metal gate. Immediately turn right down rough track to bridge over stream. Follow track left uphill and at the top bear right to gate. Follow track between fences, and pass through wooden gate onto road (171358).

Turn left uphill and then down. At sharp bend, turn right into Sene Farmhouse drive and continue straight ahead through wooden gate. Carry straight on for 25 yards. Turn left at stone wall. Continue for 25 yards with wall and trees on right. Through narrow wooden gate, along narrow track. Through wooden gate, straight across field, keeping to the right of buildings. At hard track turn left and continue downhill on army road to bridleway gate by cattle grid. Continue straight on over bridge. Straight on through tunnel under railway, and turn right towards motorway bridge. Over bridge. Through metal gate, and straight on through gateway to A20 (184372).

Turn right, then use cycle track on left hand side of road. Turn left into Danton Lane. Follow Danton Lane till T junction, then turn right following narrow road for a short distance up very steep hill. At T junction near top of hill, turn right and follow narrow busy road along the crest of the hill for about a third of a mile and take road on left. At bottom of hill opposite pond turn left onto bridleway. Continue past house and bear right along track. Carry on along track, go through wooden gate and immediately turn right, then follow track straight on passing through two wooden gates and a red iron gate. Immediately after the red iron gate follow track right, downhill through trees and up the other side. At the top of the hill, take iron gate on right. Turn left, following fence on the left to corner, then go straight across field to corner on right of trees. Carry on across the middle of the field, keeping 30 yards left of pylon. Through gateway and turn left onto track. Right at road. Left at junction.

Pass Cat and Custard Pot and Elm Cottage on right and turn right towards Acrise and Swingfield. After 100 yards, turn left through gateway with bridleway sign and go diagonally across field, keeping 20 yards left of first telegraph pole. Continue straight on to corner of field, through broken metal gate. Turn left downhill on grass verge at the side of cornfield. Through metal gate and continue in a straight line towards farm building with asbestos roof on the horizon, keeping increasingly further to the right of the fence. Through gateway next to sheep pens and follow the fence on left to farm. Through gate bear right and follow drive to road.

Turn left onto the road and carry straight on for a mile, following signposts to Etchinghill. At third junction turn right. After 20 yards, turn right down bridleway. Through metal gate, keeping fence on your left. Through second metal gate, following track through trees for about a ¼ mile and then downhill to road. At the road turn left and continue downhill to junction with main road (163407).

Turn right and then left after garage. Continue up road. Before church, follow road to right, then bear left, continuing straight at crossroads. Pass school on left and turn left at Woodland Road.

Through metal gate and along track, through hurdle. Follow track uphill. Through red metal gate left of stile leading onto wide track. Continue along the track through a second red metal gate. At the bottom of the hill follow the track round to the left to join road. Turn right, through metal gate onto road. At the junction go straight on towards Postling. Follow grass verge on left-hand side. Immediately after grass verge turn left onto track and immediately left through grey iron gate. Proceed uphill next to fence on the right. At the security fence at the top of the hill, turn left, continue to corner of the security fence and turn right through hurdles keeping the fence on your right. Turn left at the gap before first stile. Follow the track with security fence on your right and turn right at the radio mast access road and then straight on through wooden gate.

Follow concrete road. At second bend, turn left onto rutted track. At junction of paths go straight on, taking the track downhill in cutting. Follow track downhill and round to the right. Through wooden gate and follow track through cutting and through next wooden gate. Follow track along gulley with trees on either side. Turn right up the bank before next gate, and at the top of the bank turn left through the trees to grey metal gate. Carry straight on for 5 yards, turn left through narrow wooden gate and immediately right, keeping fence and then wood on your right. Through wooden gate by cattle grid. Turn left at road (150384).

Carry straight on for a short distance and at the junction with A20 turn right down bridle road next to white house. Follow the track passing through a wooden gate and a metal gate. At the end of the track, turn left through metal gate and immediately right, following fence on right of field. At the end of the field, continue straight on with dyke on left to wood. Follow the track straight on through the wood. At the far side of the wood carry straight on along narrow track between hedge and fence.

At the road (130387) turn right and continue for a short distance then turn right to Stanford North. Continue through village for a little way and just before end of cul de sac turn left up path onto motorway bridge; at bridge exit turn left onto road, which will bring you back to the start of the route.

27 Wint Hill near Weston-Super-Mare to Brockley Combe

Diana Roberts

Approx. 29k, 18 miles

OS map 182

Start: 401590:OS182

Finish: 485663:OS182

Park at Banwell in Dark Lane. Dark Lane is a quiet road running from the Folly at the top of Banwell hill to the main road between Banwell and Churchill.

Go from your box to the top of Dark Lane by the Folly. Turn right across the road and take the country lane marked Wint Hill. There are many tales told locally about murders on Wint Hill and other gruesome goings on. When you have ridden several hundred yards along the lane you will see a gate in front of you with a notice asking riders to keep to the track. Go through this gate, across the field and keep on track through copse and eventually down to the farmyard. Ride straight through farmyard and track left at tarmac lane. The M5 will be in front of and below you. Go over motorway bridge with sign 'No through road' and up stony track. When you see a small copse in front of you (called Christon Plantation) track left and go up stony track and past sunken cottage on your left. Track directly up to the right and then first left. Follow track left through iron gate with blue bridleway sign and along the track at the far left of the field right down to the road.

Go down tarmac road for about 50 yards and at junction turn right and head towards bridge over small rhyne with garage and post office just after the bridge, ignoring turning signposted for Weston and Bleadon. Continue to the left and go over motorway bridge. You are now in Somerset. You will see the Webbington Hotel in front of you and Crooks Peak towering behind the hotel. Take first turn left and ride along tarmac lane for about a mile, past house called The Paddock. You will see a track up the side of Crooks Peak marked bridleway. Follow this track up behind a luxurious house with pool and tennis courts. The hill is quite steep and pumps up the braking system for the gallop that is to follow should you so wish! There is a sign on your left indicating the direction to Shute Shelve; follow the broad turf track along towards Shute Shelve with the stone wall on your left. If you don't go fast along here you will

notice the breathtaking view around you.

The track you are on is on the main Somerset/Avon border. Continue along on this main track and you will go down into some woods; keep the wall and the large house (called The Hall) on your left. After about three minutes you will see a gate and small car park in front of you and a bridleway sign.

Turn right on the metal lane and you will immediately come to a busy junction at the A38. Be careful here; I suggest you turn left and cross over by the garage (chocolate, drinks, etc., are sold here and they are open nearly all the time). Opposite the garage you will see a stony track marked 'West Mendip Way'. Go up this track and at a junction you come to after about

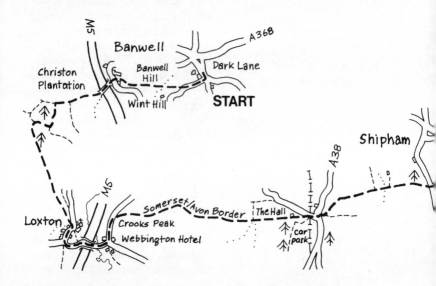

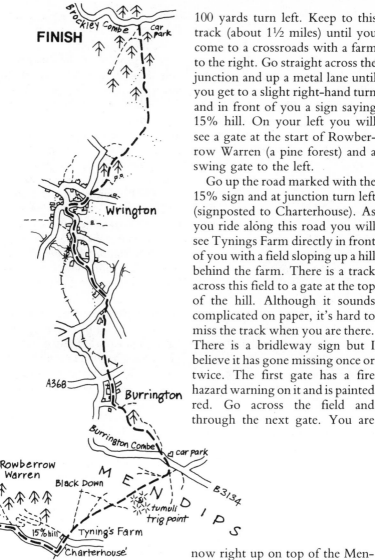

FINISH

Brockley Combe

car park

Wrington

A368

Burrington

Burrington Combe

car park

Rowberrow
Warren

Black Down

M E N D I P S

tumuli

trig point

15% hill

Tyning's Farm

Charterhouse

B3134

rm

100 yards turn left. Keep to this track (about 1½ miles) until you come to a crossroads with a farm to the right. Go straight across the junction and up a metal lane until you get to a slight right-hand turn and in front of you a sign saying 15% hill. On your left you will see a gate at the start of Rowberrow Warren (a pine forest) and a swing gate to the left.

Go up the road marked with the 15% sign and at junction turn left (signposted to Charterhouse). As you ride along this road you will see Tynings Farm directly in front of you with a field sloping up a hill behind the farm. There is a track across this field to a gate at the top of the hill. Although it sounds complicated on paper, it's hard to miss the track when you are there. There is a bridleway sign but I believe it has gone missing once or twice. The first gate has a fire hazard warning on it and is painted red. Go across the field and through the next gate. You are now right up on top of the Mendips. You will see a broad grassy track in front of you with bracken and heather on either side of you. Go along this broad path for about

30 feet and you will see the first turning on your right. Take this turning. You will see that either side of the track are barrows – small humps of earth like mole-hills. These are reputed to be markers for the drove road that used to run over Black Down. But it has also been said by locals that the barrows had trays of burning oil put on them in the last war to try and fool the Germans into thinking it was a village and dropping their bombs there instead of Chur-chill and Bristol. However, it seems that the Germans were not impressed. You will pass a trig point – drop down behind trig point on the left-hand path.

Follow this bridlepath down to the road at the top of Burrington Combe. When you reach the road go straight across to the car park and go up the left-hand bridlepath. This goes across a turfy hill and down into a small valley with a stony peak in front of you. Don't go up this hill but fork off to the right down a narrow bridlepath which threads its way through scrub and blackthorn trees. When you reach the road turn left and then at next turn go right into Burrington Village, passing the church on your left.

When you reach the main road you cannot miss a bridlepath directly in front of you – go down this bridlepath and through farm-yard onto road. Turn left and at junction fork right and go across road, following signpost for Wrington. Keep on this road and after about 10/15 minutes you will come to Wrington Village. When you reach the junc-tion in Wrington turn right to Congresbury/Yatton – then right again to Redhill/Bristol. At the top of the road (about 200 yards) go straight over by the tree to Old Hill (marked 'No through road'). Go up this hill and when you see a white gate with Barley Wood Farm sign turn left along narrow bridleway. You will soon go past a pine wood on your left and Luls-gate airport on your right. Keep straight on this path and you will come out in the famous Brockley Combe. (The car park you arrive in is well suited for parking horse boxes if you wish to start here and end in Banwell at Wint Hill).

Good Areas for Riding and Specially Devised Riding Trails

During the course of researching this book, I discovered many smaller riding routes – often created by local councils for walkers and riders out of old railways lines – and also many country parks where riding is allowed. They are *not* comprehensive, and you may well discover others. They are given below under areas: The North, The Midlands and East Anglia, Wales and the Borders, the West Country and the South. Where a leaflet is available, I have given the address from which to obtain it; in many cases, permits are required, and addresses for application are given. I have not given fees, since these are subject to change.

The best providers of areas for riding are the Forestry Commission and the Water Authorities in each region. The Forestry Commission is charged with providing access to the countryside, and in some forests they have set aside special riding trails, well marked, for which you need a permit. The addresses of Forestry Commission regional offices are given below.

Some forests allow unrestricted riding, provided the chief forester is happy that there is no danger from felling; in other forests there are specified trails, which may be closed temporarily due to erosion. Maps are usually available for these.

To obtain a permit you must fill out a form which demands that you take out an insurance policy for not less than £100,000 in respect of any one claim to cover any injury or damage caused by your action. They may ask to see the policy and the receipt for your last premium. Don't panic – first find out if your householders' policy covers you against such claims; it quite likely will.

North East Region
1A Grosvenor Terrace
York
Tel. (0904) 20221

(for Northumberland, Tyne & Wear,
Durham, Cleveland, North West and
South Yorkshire, North Humberside.

East Region
Government Buildings
Brooklands Avenue
Block D
Cambridge
Tel. (0223) 58911

(for Lincolnshire, South Humberside,
Norfolk, Suffolk, Essex,
Hertfordshire, Buckinghamshire,
Northamptonshire, Oxfordshire,
Leicestershire (Rutland))

South East Region
The Queen's House
Lyndhurst
Tel. (042–128) 2801

(for Hampshire, Isle of Wight,
Berkshire, Surrey, Kent, Sussex,
Dorset (South East))

South West Region
Flowers Hill
Brislington
Bristol
Tel. (0272) 713471

(for Cornwall, Devon, Somerset,
Avon, Gloucestershire, Wiltshire,
Dorset (West), Hereford & Worcester
(South))

North West Region
Dee Hills Park
Chester
Tel. (0244) 24006

(for Cumbria, Lancashire, Derbyshire,
Nottinghamshire, Cheshire, Salop,
Staffordshire, West Midlands,
Warwickshire, Hereford & Worcester
(North))

North Wales
Victoria House
Victoria Terrace
Aberystwyth
Tel. (0970) 612367

South Wales
Churchill House
Churchill Way
Cardiff
Tel. (0222) 40661

Scotland
North:
21 Church Street
Inverness 1V1 1EL
Tel. (0463) 32811

South:
Greystone Park
55/57 Moffat Road
Dumfries DG1 1NP
Tel. (0387) 2425

East:
6 Queen's Gate
Aberdeen AB9 2NQ
Tel. (0224) 33361

West:
Portcullis House
21 India Street
Glasgow G2 4PL
Tel. (041–248) 3931

THE NORTH

Runcorn Town Park Bridleway, Cheshire
9k, 5½ miles
Bridleway indicated by markers.
Access at any point where public access is possible.
Park Rangers patrol the parks and bridleway, organize a wide range of events and activities for all ages.

Information:
   The Rangers Office
   Stockham Lane
   Runcorn
   Tel. (0928) 719453
Leaflet available

Wirral Way Horse Ride, Merseyside
1. West Kirby to Thurstaston: 4k, 2½ miles
2. Thurstaston to Blackwood Hall Lane, Parkgate: 5.6k, 3½ miles
3. Backwood Hall Lane, Parkgate, to Lees Lane, Neston: 5.6k, 3½ miles
4. Lees Lane, Neston, to Hooton: 4k, 2½ miles
Car parks at Sandy Lane, West Kirby, Croft Drive, Caldy, Banks Road, Thurstaston, Parkgate Old Baths, Heswall, Lees Lane, Neston, Hadlow Road Station, Willaston. The Wirral Way leads (15k, 9½ miles) to the coast, cutting through the town park and residential areas. The horse ride runs parallel to the walk for much of the way – along an old railway line.

Information:
   Wirral Country Park Centre
   Station Road
   Thurstaston
   Wirral
   Merseyside L61 0HN
   Tel. (051) 648 4371

Leaflet from:
   Countryside Division of Cheshire
   County Council
   County Hall
   Chester CH1 1SF

Craik Forest, Scottish Borders
Two riding trails
6.4k, 4 miles and 14.4k, 9 miles
Horsebox area in main car park
Open: Easter to October 31st; other times by arrangement with conservator
Tickets to be purchased
Restrictions: avoid breaking up routes by cantering or galloping

Information:
   Forester in charge
   Craik Forest
   Hawick
   Tel. (045 088) 282
      or
   Conservator
   Forestry Commission
   55 Moffat Rd
   Dumfries
   Tel. (0387) 69171
Leaflet available

Hawick Circular Ride, Borders
43k, 27 miles
Connected riding trails, waymarked with blue arrows
Restrictions: no cantering or galloping

Information:
   Countryside Ranger
   Borders Regional Council
   Planning Department
   Regional Headquarters
   Newtown St Boswells
   Tel. (0835) 23301

Railway walks in County Durham

Various walking/riding routes on old
railway lines
Waskerley Way: 9.6k, 6½ miles
Derwent Valley: 16.8k, 10½ miles
Brandon–Bishop Auckland: 15.2k, 9½
miles
Lanchester Valley: 19.2k, 12 miles
Deerness Valley: 11.2k, 7 miles
Restrictions: horses may only be walked

Information:
  Durham County Planning
  Department
  County Hall
  Durham City DH1 5UF
  Tel. (0385) 64411 X 2594
Leaflets available

Derwent Walk Country Park

Bridleway along old railway track
Car parks at Shotley Bridge, Ebchester
Station, High Hamsterley, Rowlands
Gill and Swalwell Station

Information:
  County Planning Department
  County Hall
  Durham DH1 5UF
  Tel. (0385) 64411 X 354
Leaflet available

MIDLANDS AND EAST ANGLIA

Sutton Park, Birmingham

Bridleway experiment
Horsebox parking at Barriers Gate
entrance, Boldmere Gate and near
railway by Streetly entrance

Information:
  Department of Recreation and
  Community Services
  Auchinleck House
  Five Ways
  Birmingham B15 1DS
  Tel. (021) 235 9944
Map available

Sandwell Wedge Bridleway, West Midlands

11.2k, 7 miles
Information:
  County Planning Department
  County Hall
  Lancaster Circus
  Queensway
  Birmingham B4 7DJ

Epping Forest, Essex
Various horse trails, no charge
Restrictions: certain areas may be closed
because of heavy erosion
Parking: during daylight hours;
horseboxes at Sudbury Farm car park,
Oak Hill car park, near the Information
Centre, Strawberry Hill, Fairmead
pond, near Chingford Station, Rangers
Road, Hollow Pond, Wanstead Flats
and Alexandra Lake

Information:
   Conservators of Epping Forest
   The Warren
   Loughton
   Essex IG10 4RW
   Tel. (01) 508 2266
Map available

Weald Country Park, Essex
3.2k, 2 mile riding trail, plus 86 acres of
free riding, except after 10 a.m. on
weekends
Temporary exclusions because of
erosion
Restrictions: cantering and galloping only
where indicated
Permits only
Horseboxes in car park 1
Open: from 7 a.m. to half an hour after
sunset

Information:
   Parks Office
   Weald Country Park
   South Weald
   Brentwood
   Essex
   Tel. (0277) 216297

Langdon Hills (East) Country Park, Essex
Horse rides in East Mersea, and
Thorndon Country Park
Permit required

Information:
   Country Estates Officer and Valuer
   Clarendon House
   Parkway
   Chelmsford CH2 0NT

River Mardyke, Essex
17.6k, 11 mile ride along the banks of
the river from its confluence with the
River Thames
Route being developed by Thurrock
Borough Council

Information:
   Council Offices
   Whitehall Lane
   Grays
   Essex RM17 6SL
   Tel. (0375) 5122

Bradgate Park, Charnwood Forest, Leicestershire
Riding trails which are subject to change
to prevent erosion

Information:
   Planning Department
   Leicestershire County Council
   County Hall
   Glenfield
   Leicester LE3 8RJ
   Tel. (0533) 871313
Map available

Henham Park, Suffolk
Riding routes signposted with arrows
Permit required

Apply to:
  The Secretary
  Henham Estate Office
  Wargford
  Beccles
  Suffolk
  Tel. (050 278) 212

Thornham Park, Thornham Magna, Eye, Suffolk
System of bridleways
Annual permit
Also permanent cross-country course
on the estate and area suitable for
dressage and show-jumping

Information:
  Mrs Popescu
  The Old Parsonage
  Mellis
  Eye
  Suffolk

Park Hall Country Park, Staffordshire
Riding trail
Permit required

Information:
  Staffordshire County Planning
  Department
  County Buildings
  Martin St
  Stafford ST16 2LE
Leaflet available

Rutland Water, Northants
Anglian Water Authority
Riding track
Horsebox parking at car parks (fee
payable)

Information:
  Anglian Water
  North St
  Oundle
  Peterborough PE8 4AS
  Tel. (0832) 73701
Leaflet available

Wimpole Way, Cambridgeshire
17.6k, 11 miles
near Wimpole Hall (National Trust)
Riding trail

Information:
  Rights of Way Officer
  Cambridge County Council
  Shire Hall
  Cambridge CB3 0AP
  Tel. (0223) 317721

Grafham Water, off A1, Cambridgeshire
19.2k, 12 miles
Riding trail around reservoir
Horsebox parking at car parks

Thetford Forest, Norfolk
Various good riding trails
Permit required
Santon Downham, Bridgham, Harling
Riding Trail and Thetford Chase

Applications and information:
  Forestry Commission
  Santon Downham
  Brandon
  Norfolk

Drayton to Attlebridge, nr
Norwich, Norfolk
(Marriott's Way)
11.2k, 7 mile railway route for riders
and walkers
No galloping on soft sandy areas
Access: Freeland Corner, Lodge Farm
and Drayton

Information:
County Planning Department
Norfolk County Council
County Hall
Martineau Lane
Norwich NR1 2DH
Tel. (0603) 611122
Leaflet available

WALES AND THE BORDERS

Pembrokeshire Coast National Park
Riding is permitted throughout the park
except the offshore islands where there
are no horses anyway. The most
popular areas are beaches (crown
foreshore) and the Presceli Hills
(common land). However, a bye-law
has been drafted (and may now be in
force) to restrict times when beach
riding is allowed – it would operate
during the spring and bank holiday
weeks and the months of July and
August from 10 a.m.–5 p.m.

Information centres:
Kingsmoor Common
Kilgetty
Tel. (0834) 812175

40 High St
Haverfordwest
Tel. (0437) 66141

Drill Hall
Main St
Pembroke
Tel. (0646) 2148

The Norton
Tenby
(0834) 3510

The City Hall
St David's
Tel. (0437) 392

Carn Ingli Centre
East St
Newport
(0239) 820912

On National Car Park
Broad Haven
(043 783) 412

Main Information Centre:
Head Ranger
County Offices
Haverfordwest
Dyfed SA61 1QZ
Tel. (0437) 3131
Leaflet available

Tintern South Riding Circuit
Forestry Commission
8k, 5 miles
Through Bishop's Barnets Wood and
Pierre's Great Wood, with connecting
routes through Kites Bushes and
Cockshoots Woods
South-west of Chepstow
Two signposted entrances to Bishop's
Barnets Wood: on B4235, approx. ¼
mile west of Crossway Green,
Chepstow, the other past Barnets Wood
picnic site, ½ mile further west on same
road.
Route waymarked with horseshoe
symbols. Where the route runs
alongside the road, the verge has been
cleared and riders are advised to use
verge.
Permit required

Information:
    Crown Lodge
    Tintern
    Tel. (029 18) 212

Chepstow Park Wood riding circuit
8k, 5½ miles
5 miles north-west of Chepstow
Two signposted entrances: on B4293
1¾ miles beyond St Arvans in
Debauden direction where there is hard
standing outside barrier, where
horseboxes may be parked. Other
entrance 1 mile beyond Itton on Itton-
Devauden road. This entrance for riders
only.
Waymarked route with horseshoe
symbols.
Permit required

Information and applications to:
    Forestry Commission
    Crown Office
    Tintern
    Tel. (029 18) 212

THE WEST COUNTRY

The obvious ones are Dartmoor and
Exmoor, where, apart from the
recognized bridleways you can, with
care, ride almost anywhere

Exmoor Information:
    Exmoor National Park
    Exmoor House
    Dulverton
    Somerset TA22 9HL
    Tel. (0398) 23665

Dartmoor Information:
    National Park Office
    Parke
    Haytor Road
    Bovey Tracey
    Newton Abbot
    Devon TQ13 9JQ
    Tel. (0626) 832093

Wadebridge Padstow Path
9k, 5½ miles
Disused railway line

Information:
 Cornwall County Planning
 Department
 County Hall
 Truro TR1 3BB
 Tel. (0872) 74282
Leaflet available

Cirencester Park, Gloucester
A grass and woodland ride
No horseboxes in park
Restrictions: no jumping, cantering or galloping

Information:
 Bathhurst Estate
 Estate Office
 Cirencester Park
 Cirencester GL7 2BU
 Tel. (0285) 3135

THE SOUTH

Ringwood Forest, Hampshire
Permits available for some tracks.
Information as below

Queen Elizabeth Country Park, Hampshire
Forest bridle tracks may be used without charge. Horses may be hired from stables in forest
Horsebox parking: Gravel Hill Car Park (beyond Park Centre)
When ground damp, only walking allowed, no galloping
Leaflet available

West Walk, Bere Forest
Extensive network of bridle tracks
Permit required

Lords Wood, Rownhams Chilworth
Various bridle tracks
Permit required

Information:
 Ringwood Forest Office
 Horton Rd
 Ashley Heath
 Ringwood
 Hants
 Tel. (04254) 5656

Queen Elizabeth Forest Office:
 Buriton
 Petersfield
 Hants GU31 5SL
 Tel. (0730) 63482

Upper Hamble Country Park, Hampshire

Riding tracks marked with horseshoe symbol, easily identified by yellow gravel surface
Permissive tracks may be changed or closed when too wet
Restrictions: no galloping. Cantering only when visibility good. Walking only when ground wet

Information:
    County Recreation Department
    Hampshire County Council
    North Hill Close
    Winchester
    Hampshire
    Tel. (0962) 64221

New Forest

Riding is permitted on the Forestry Commission land and on trails and rides in Inclosures
No charge

Information:
    Forestry Commission
    Queen's House
    Lyndhurst
    Hampshire SO4 7NH
    Tel. (042 128) 2801
Map available

Binfield Bridleway Circuit, Bracknell, Berkshire

16k, 10 miles
A circuit of signposted bridleway and road with two loops, each five miles long

Information:
    Recreation Department
    Tel. (0344) 24642
Leaflet available

Frensham Country Park, Surrey

Definitive bridleways and permissive bridleways
Blackheath Common, Surrey

Information:
    Waverley District Council
    The Burys
    Godalming
    Surrey GU7 1HR
    Tel. (04868) 4104
Leaflet available

Bramshill Forest, Surrey

Crowthorne Wood, Garrick Woods, Bramshill Common, Heath Warren, Warren Heath, Eversley Common
Horse trails
Permit required

Information:
    Bramshill Forest Office
    Blackwater
    Camberley
    Surrey GU17 9LB
    Tel. (0252) 872154

Ruislip Woods, London Borough of Hillingdon

Copse Wood, Mad Bess Wood, Bayhurst Wood, Country Park, Park Wood
Horsebox parking at Bayhurst Wood off Breakspear Road North and Mad Bess Wood, off Duck's Hill Road
Condition of bridleways a problem because heavy clay though they've tried to improve the surface by applying sand and woodchips

Information:
    Leisure Services Dept
    London Borough of Hillingdon
    Civic Centre
    Uxbridge
    Middlesex UB8 1UW
Leaflet available

Toys Hill Woodlands, near Westerham, Kent

National Trust
Permissive bridleways waymarked in blue, with various circular tracks linked with public bridleways
No horseboxes in car parks

Information:
  National Trust Regional Office
  Tel. (0892) 890651

Challock Forest, Kent

Kings Wood, Clowes Wood, Denge Wood, Covet Wood, Covwer Wood, Madams Wood, Elham Park Wood, Park Wood, Beveridge Wood, West Wood, Joydens Wood, High Chart Wood, Meenfield Wood
Riding trails
Permit required

Information:
  Head Forester
  Forest Office
  Challock
  Ashford
  Kent TN25 4AR
  Tel. (023374) 420

Ashdown Forest, Sussex

Permit required

Information:
  Clerk to Conservators of Ashdown Forest
  Village Hall
  Forest Row
  Tel. (034 282) 3583

Bedgebury Forest, Sussex

Flimwell, Hemsted, Snape Wood, Coombe Complex, Brightling Down, Deer Park Complex, Darwell Woods, Great Woods, Bixley Wood, Brassets Wood, Beckley Complex, Friston Forest, Wilmington Forest, St Leonards Forest, Tilgate Forest, Gravetye Forest,

Sheffield Forest
Riding trails
Permit required

Information:
  Chief Forester
  Forest Lodge
  Netherfield Down
  Battle
  E. Sussex TN33 9PX
  Tel. (04246) 2730
Maps available

Forest Way, Sussex/Kent

15½k, 9½ miles
Disused railway line between Groombridge and East Grinstead
Access: B2110 Edenbridge-Withyham Rd, B2026, A22 at Forest Row, Luxford Lane

Information:
  County Planning Department
  Southover House
  Southover Road
  Lewes
Leaflet available

Bewl Bridge Reservoir, Lamberhurst, Kent

Southern Water Authority
25.6k, 16 miles
Bridleways marked with blue arrows. Circular route round reservoir, which you must leave for a short section. Certain sections are permissive and during bad weather these sections can be closed due to mud. Advisable in bad weather conditions to phone reservoir recreation office to check
Entrance off A21 London-Hastings road, 1 mile south of Lamberhurst
Horseboxes to public car parks; use parking area designated for horseboxes
There is a charge for using car parks
Restrictions: no galloping, cantering only when you can see ahead

Open:
    April–mid October 24 hours
    Mid October–April 9 a.m.–sunset
    Closed Christmas Day
    Permit required

Information:
    Manager
    Bewl Bridge Reservoir
    Lamberhurst
    Tunbridge Wells
    Kent
    Tel. (0892) 890661
Leaflet available

ISLE OF WIGHT

Long Distance Trails
Five very good long distance trails
waymarked with red paint, composed
of footpaths, bridleways and ancient
highways, linked with short sections of
road (these are the only routes possible
for riders – there are more for walkers)

Tennyson Trail
4k, 15 miles
Large parts of this are bridleway but not
the beginning
Nodgham Lane, Carisbrooke, to Alum
Bay
Open: all year, with downland, marine
views and forest

Worsley Trail
24k, 15 miles
Large parts of this are bridleway with
diversion to Shanklin
Shanklin Old Village to Brighstone
Forest
Open: all year, pine forest, high
countryside and downland

Stenbury Trail
16k, 10 miles
Large parts of this are bridleway, but not
the end
Blackwater, near Newport to Week
Down, Ventnor
Open: all year, with pine forest, high
countryside and downland

Nunwell Trail
16k, 10 miles
Again, large parts are bridleway but not
the end of the route
Ryde, St John's Station, to Sandown
Station
Open: all year, with mixed country,
downland, water meadows

Shepherd's Trail
16k, 10 miles
Mostly bridleway
Whitcombe Cross, Carisbrooke, to
Shepherds Chine, Atherfield
Open: all year, with high ground,
downland, views

*An excellent series of leaflets and maps are
available from*:
    Isle of Wight County Council
    County Hall
    Newport
    Isle of Wight PO30 1UD
    Tel. (0983) 524031

Law and Lore
on Rights of Way

In common with the best fairy stories, local folklore has it that 'Once upon a time' there were routes to travel from 'A' to 'B' on horseback, but that nowadays – somehow – these have been lost, stolen or strayed so that, just like the other old fairy paths, they are elusive and inaccessible to ordinary mortals.

Many riders will recognize in the story their own experiences: unnumerable byways and bridleways have been lost in the past for various reasons ranging from non-registration to misregistration, ploughing-up to deliberate obstruction, or simply because they have not been maintained. The fact that only too many Highway Authorities have utterly failed to carry out the legal obligations or duties imposed on them by both Common Law and various Acts of Parliament to keep rights of way open is a contributory factor that has compounded the above wrongs.

The result is to force horse and rider on to the lethal main roads, where their lives are at risk every time they leave field or stable; the problem for most riders is to know how to retain or improve a network of safe riding routes.

While there are several possible answers to this question, there is just one basic one. *You* have to do something, either individually or by joining an organization (national or local) which promotes the same aims. However, you can only be effective, or help any organization, if you are aware of your rights under the present law and can use them to remedy the wrongs outlined above. Even in cases where a direct friendly approach to a landowner is possible, a sure knowledge of exactly how matters stand in regard to the responsibilities of Highway Authorities, landowner or tenant, and user can help you make your case without being belligerent and may just tip the scales in the right direction. If a friendly approach is unsuccessful, or obviously not going to be so, then other steps have to be taken; but no County Council, District Council or Parish Council will take any action unless firmly, repeatedly and persistently pushed into it by a member of the public.

The following pages can give only a general guide and brief outline of the most important facts you ought to know, and some indication as to future actions you may need to take. Precise and more detailed information can be obtained from the list of specialized books (some written especially for the layman) given at the end of this section, or through the organizations whose names and addresses are also given there. Particularly recommended is *Rights of Way. A Guide to Law and Practice* by Paul Clayden and John Trevelyan, which is very reasonably priced considering the vast amount of detail it offers in regard to both Common and Statutory Law.

Three vital facts

1.   *Definitive maps.* Public rights of way include footpaths, bridleways and byways. All these are (or should be) registered and shown on a special map known as a Definitive Map, a copy of which will be held by the relevant County Council to cover all the parishes within its area, each District Council for its own parishes, and individual parishes for that parish only. The general public has the right to inspect any Definitive Map held by a particular authority during office hours, or possibly by convenient arrangement with a parish clerk who works from a home base.

However, the fact that a route is not shown on the map does not necessarily mean it does not exist. It does mean that anyone claiming a path of whatever status has to provide the evidence to substantiate his claim (which often is proof of a historical right of way or highway).

The different types of rights of way will usually be shown on the Definitive Map by the use of standard conventional symbols, though some may use coloured lines instead (WCA 1981 Regulations, 1983. Schedule 1.) Annexed to the Definitive Map should be a separate 'Statement', on which is a written description of the line of the path from one end to the other, often including details of the length, width, right to plough, etc.

The following are definitions of the various paths and the rights attached to each status.

Footpath (FP)   A right of way on foot only, unless an individual has been given permission to pass through in any other way by the landowner. (WCA 1981. S.66)

Bridleway (BR)   A right of way on foot, riding or leading a horse or possibly driving cattle. Motorized invalid carriages can also use BRs, as can pedal cycles. Other methods with the landowner's permission only. (WCA 1981. S.66)

Byway (RUPP) (BY) (BOAT)   Originally, these were termed 'Roads used as Public Paths' (RUPPs), being *'other* than bridleways and footpaths' such as old green lanes or unmetalled roads, which may or may not have been old cart tracks (i.e. vehicular roads). All of these can be ridden. This led to confusion, since people were unaware of their exact rights. Since 1968, the government has instructed county councils to decide whether vehicles do hold historical rights over particular RUPPs, and to rename and register them either as 'byways open to all traffic' (BOATs) or bridleways, as appropriate. (WCA 1981. S.54)

It is now possible to alter both map and statement from time to time; the alterations to the RUPPs are called reclassifications, but other changes to public paths for whatever reasons are called modifications. Both must be advertised in the local paper as a 'Definitive Map Order' (DMO) and riders should always watch out for them. They could affect your riding rights in your own area! (WCA 1981. S.53)

2.   *Conclusive evidence.* Where a right of way is shown on such a map, it is legal and conclusive evidence that a right of way of a particular status existed at the time the current map was published, and that the public hold just as much right to pass over them (according to the rights allotted to them) as along any main or metalled road used by vehicles. (WCA 1981. S.56) Ordnance Survey maps do indicate rights of way but cannot be relied on as being completely up to date. Even so, this absolute right will not absolve the responsible user from the obligations of observing the 'rules of the road' such as courtesy, care and consideration for other users, and the landowner.

3.   *Duties, powers and responsibilities.* Under the Highways Act, 1980, Section I, the County Council was designated as the highway authority for its own area, and thus made responsible for all rights of way. 'Duty' is a word which means that the County Council *must* carry out the actions it is ordered to perform, as opposed to the word 'power' which indicates an option to undertake certain acts if it so wishes. The following is perhaps the most important example: 'It is the *duty* of a County Council to assert and protect the rights of the public to the use and enjoyment of, and to prevent as far as possible the stopping up or obstruction of, all highways for which they are the Highway Authority'. (Highways Act, 1980. Section 130) (My italics)

There are various other duties and powers allocated to County Councils, including delegation of some powers to District Councils, but this will be dealt with later on. Delegation does not take away the final responsibility of the County Council for all its highways.

Definitive maps and the recording of rights of way

In 1949 the government enacted the National Parks and Access to the Countryside Act, so that a record could be made of rights of way in England and Wales (not Scotland). County Councils were supposed to complete the task by the early 1950s, and thereafter review their Definitive Map every five years by amending wrongly recorded paths or deleting them, or adding new or unregistered old tracks.

A forlorn hope indeed. Some counties had not produced a Definitive Map of any sort right up to the 1970s. Others had never reviewed or revised their original map whatever date it was published; a few had done at least one five-yearly review and were perhaps in the throes of a second one when the emergence of the Countryside Act 1968 stopped such activities dead in their tracks. Under this Act, briefly, counties had to start again, but reclassifying all 'Roads used as Public Paths' under new headings as either a 'byway open to all traffic' or as a bridleway, in a complicated system involving one of two methods (Special or General), and followed by time-consuming public inquiries which frequently took anything up to eight years to happen. And some of those inquiries have never taken place at all, as of 1986. Those that did then waited several years before the Secretary of State (through his legal body of the Department of the Environment, the DOE) advised the county council of his decisions on the matter, after which the CC refused to take any action on any changes or additions until it was able to publish a new Definitive Map which would cover the complete county.

Between the National Parks and Access to the Countryside Act of 1949 and the Countryside Act of 1968 were twenty years of neglect and chaos, followed by a similar pattern for another twenty odd years until the Wildlife and Countryside Act of 1981, at which time a few counties still had not produced a complete Definitive Map in forty years, and all counties were further disorganized by the local government reorganization in 1974.

It is difficult to imagine *any* other area of Statutory Law which could have been so negligently disregarded and disobeyed by responsible authorities, and malfeasance equally calmly condoned by successive governments. It is not difficult to imagine the numbers of knowledgeable witnesses alive before 1900 and up to 1949 or later who had presented claims to rights of way of all statuses who have died, moved out of the area, or are now too feeble to come forward, who have never had those claims considered; nor to guess at the innumerable numbers of bridleways and byways lost in this manner.

The Wildlife and Countryside Act of 1981 changed the rules for making, reviewing and amending Definitive Maps, and has further delayed the completion of new and accurate up-to-date maps. Many counties which did at least have a complete map in the past do not, in 1986, now hold a new map incorporating all the legal changes or reclassifications which have taken place since 1949, or have even completed the coverage of such changes for the whole county. This, they estimate, will take many more years yet.

The main change in the 1981 Act was to legalize a continuous, ongoing review system by the County Councils instead of a (supposedly) five-yearly interval, by means of Definitive Map Orders (DMOs), so that County Councils now have a *duty* to bring the map and statement up to date, and then keep them up to date. A DMO can be presented to the CC by any member of the public.

However, the 1981 Act S.53 contains the ominous words 'as soon as reasonably practical', and it remains to be seen how the County Councils interpret them.

What the Act does do is to place the onus of finding and proving the correct status of missing or misregistered routes, or of 20 years usage, squarely on the shoulders of the general public. Moreover, forwarding a request for a DMO to the Highway Authority for acceptance has to be done in a standard procedure, on standard forms. Copies of these forms and the requirements contained therein are placed after this section, and are self-explanatory, but the Act and Circular should be consulted for full instructions and details of how the new system works. The public should not be put off by its apparent complexity from seeking to extend of regain bridleways. Information on where to search for acceptable evidence will be available in another section.

General information

1. *Common and statutory law.* Laws regarding highways have come down to us throughout recorded history, and have changed from time to time as circumstances altered. Although the changes were made under individual Acts of Parliament, every now and then such new, amended or repealed legislation was gathered together in a 'Consolidated' Act of up-to-date law, usually known as 'The Highway Act' of whatever year it was published in.

The more recent individual Acts that have affected rights of way are:

(i)   The National Parks and Access to the Countryside Act, 1949. (NPAC 1949)

(ii)   The Countryside Act, 1968. (CA 1968)

(iii)   The Town and Country Planning Act, 1971. (TCPA 1971)

(iv)   The Local Government Act, 1972. (LGA 1972)

(v)   The Highways Act, 1980. (HA 1980)

(vi)   The Wildlife and Countryside Act, 1981. (WCA 1981)

Generally speaking, the latest Highway Act to have been issued is the one to look at, plus any later Act which may have amended or added to rights of way laws. When a new Act is published it is usual for an official 'circular' to be sent out with it, which expands and clarifies into layman's terms the contents of the Act, making it easier to understand. Read this first, before looking at the Act itself. The circular sent out with the WCA 1981 (DOE Circular 1/83) is particularly important. (Note:- in older acts, the circular was called a memorandum instead.)

2. *Judicial law.* The judgements given in various court cases hold for future similar cases and are frequently reflected in subsequent legislation. An excellent example is the 'Hood' case, in which the judges laid down that no RUPP could be reclassified as *less* than a bridleway except under some very exceptional circumstances.

Duties of the Highway Authority (i.e. The County Council)
(i)   To keep the Definitive Map under continuous review, and bring it up to date when reclassifications or modifications have been ratified. Both of the latter must be published in the local press before they can be ratified; the public can then object if the proposal merits such an action. (WCA 1981. S.53)

(ii)   To keep copies of the Definitive Map and statement available for public inspection as widely as possible (at a minimum at County Headquarters, District Council Offices and Parish Council Offices), plus recent Definitive Map orders. The County Council should also inform the public of its right to make applications for DMOs on its own behalf. (WCA 1981. S.57)

(iii)   To protect the right of the public to use rights of way, and keep them open for use. (HA 1980. S.130)

(iv)   To keep an up-to-date list of highways maintainable at public expense, and also to make that list available for inspection at each District Council. (HA 1980. S.36)

(v)   To maintain those highways that are maintainable at public expense (including all public rights of way). (HA 1980. S.41 and 42)

(vi)   To signpost footpaths, bridleways and byways where they join a metalled road (unless the Parish Council deems this unnecessary), and to waymark (where necessary) along the route to guide strangers who might otherwise become lost. (CA 1968. S.27)

(vii)   To prosecute anyone putting a 'misleading notice' on or near a right of way likely to deter a legitimate user from taking that route (e.g. a footpath sign at the beginning of a bridleway, etc.). (NPAC 1949. S.57)

(viii)   To negotiate with District Councils (DCs) what powers they could take over as agents for the County Council (CC), such as maintenance of footpaths and bridleways, and the making of public path orders. Although the DCs may take over certain responsibilities, this does not absolve the CC from the final responsibility for its own rights of way. (LGA 1972. S.101) Since district councils do make public path orders (for planning purposes) under the Town and Country Planning Act, 1971, it is as well to keep a careful check on the 'Official Notices' section of local newspapers. (TCPA 1971. S.210 and 214) Some of the national parks also have Planning Boards which may accept the powers accorded by the CC to DCs.

(ix)   Carry out the DUTY to provide an adequate grass verge or other margin alongside a carriageway when necessary or desirable for safety of ridden horses (HA 1980 571)

In connection with (iii) above, the Highway Authority holds two methods of dealing with an obdurate offender who has ignored all previous directions to remove obstructions. It can:

(i)   Prosecute the offender in court. (HA 1980. S.137)

(ii)   Remove the obstruction itself, and charge the offender for expenses incurred. (HA 1980. S.143) If the offence consists of anything deposited on a highway causing a nuisance which is not removed 'forthwith' the Highway Authority can also remove it themselves and recover the cost. (HA 1980. S.149)

Parish Councils are also allocated some useful powers in their own right, as follows, and should be pressed to use them when required:

A Parish Council can:

(i)   Inform the County Council that a right of way (RoW) has been unlawfully stopped up or obstructed. The Highways Authority must then act under their duty to do so. (HA 1980. S.130).

(ii)   Prosecute in its own right anyone who obstructs a RoW so that it cannot be used. (HA 1980. S.137)

(iii)   In the same way, prosecute anyone who unlawfully ploughs up a RoW or, where there is a common law right to plough a RoW, the path has not been restored for use by the authorized time limit. (HA 1980. S.134)

(iv)   Veto the action of the County Council when it proposes to apply to a magistrates court to stop up or divert a RoW. (HA 1980. S.116)

(v)   Insist that a RoW must be signposted where it joins a metalled road (CA 1968. S.27), and also signpost and waymark RoW as approved agents of the County Council. (CA 1968. S.27)

(vi)   Should be consulted by the Highway Authority before a Definitive Map Order (DMO) is made, and the Parish Council can object to such an order either under reclassification or modification. It must always receive a copy of the DMO, both when made or confirmed. (WCA 1981. Schedules 14 and 15) and (HA 1980. Schedule 6)

(vii)   Undertake certain powers in connection with the maintenance of the RoW in its parish, including lighting them or putting up notices warning of danger. (HA 1980. S.43 and S.50) and (Parish Councils Act 1957. S.3) and (Parish Councils and Burial Authorities (Miscellaneous Provisions) Act, 1970. S.3)

(viii) Negotiate with landowners over the possible creation of new footpaths and bridleways. (HA 1980. S.30)

Most Parish Councils have a separate committee which, for unknown reasons, is always referred to as 'The Footpath Committee' as if no other RoW ever existed. Perhaps Parish Councils could be persuaded to correct this misnomer and rechristen their committees as 'the Rights of Way Committees'.

Be that as it may, it is courteous to forward a copy of any letter of complaint in regard to RoW sent to the Highway Authority to your Parish Council also. Local influence exerted by a conscientious council can be very helpful, particularly with a tactful approach to the landowner concerned. Failing that, the PC can always go directly to the CC under the terms set out in (i) above.

Obstructions and Nuisances

These are difficult to define separately, since some nuisances once listed under common law are now offences incorporated in statutory law. The following items are generally regarded as offences which can be quoted to the Highway Authority, and redress applied for whatever the official heading.

As mentioned before these notes are very broadly based and curtailed, and as various provisos can qualify the meaning of the word 'offence', this should be checked with the County Council or against the Act given as reference.

(i)   To wilfully obstruct the free passage along a highway . . . is an offence. (HA 1980. S.137) Obstruction can range from actually barring the route to vocal intimidation or the use of fierce dogs, etc.

(ii)   To construct a ditch or excavation on a highway, or remove soil or turf.
        To deposit anything on a highway that damages it.
        To deposit anything on a highway to the interruption of any user of the highway. (HA 1980. S.148)
        To deposit anything which causes a user to be injured or endangered.
        To allow any filth, dirt, lime or any other offensive thing to run or flow onto a highway from adjoining premises. (HA 1980. S.161)
        To encroach on wayside waste which is part of a highway. (HA 1980. S.130)

(iii)   To place a misleading notice on or near a right of way which may deter a user from doing so. (NPAC 1949. S.57)
        To pull down or obliterate a traffic sign, milestone or direction post. (HA 1980. S.131)

To place unauthorized signs of any sort on or near a highway. (HA 1980. S.132)

(iv)   To plough a RoW which runs along the headland or sides of a field, or not to restore the line of the path (after permitted ploughing) within the time limit, which is normally two weeks.

It is illegal to plough a RUPP or byway under any circumstances. (WCA 1981. S.61).

(v)   To have on adjoining land barbed wire which is a nuisance to the highway. (Barbed wire *across* the RoW is an obstruction, of course). (HA 1980. S.164)

To place rope or wire across a highway to the danger of a user. (HA 1980. S.162)

(vi)   To have a gate across a bridleway which measures less than 5 feet wide between the gateposts. (HA 1980. S.145)

To have a gate or other structure across a bridleway in an unsafe condition which presents unreasonable interference to a user. (This presumably means the frequently met 'lash-up' of wire, stick and string is illegal under the heading of 'structure'.) (HA 1980. S.146)

It has been traditionally accepted that a rider on a bridleway should be able to open and shut a gate without dismounting, and this axiom is now presumably covered by the phrase 'a standard of repair required to prevent unreasonable interference with the rights of persons using the footpath or bridleway'. (CA 1968. S.28)

(vii)   To drive a motor vehicle (including a motor bike) along a bridleway without the express permission of the landowner. (Road Traffic Act 1972. S.36)

To hold trials of motor vehicles over a bridleway without prior permission from both the Highway Authority and the landlowner. (RTA 1972. S.35)

The Highway Authority must also give its permission before trials are held on RUPPs or byways.

(viii)   To permit a bull in a field containing a RoW, when it is over ten months old and belongs to a recognized dairy breed. However, a beef bull, accompanied by cows and heifers, is so permitted. (WCA 1981. S.59)

To allow to be, unrestrained, an animal known to have danger-ous propensities in a field with a RoW. This includes 'an animal not normally dangerous . . . except at particular times or in particular circumstances' and this, presumably, would apply to a stallion or rig, or boar pig. (Animals Act 1971. S.2)

(ix)   To light a fire or discharge a gun within 50 feet of the centre of a *carriageway*. (HA 1980. S.131)

Immediate action on meeting obstruction on rights of way

In common law, the public has only the right to 'pass and repass' over a highway, though it may *reasonably* pause, sit down for a rest, and so on. However, the public should not be 'unlawfully' or 'wilfully' obstructed while doing so, and if one finds anything which impedes passage it is permitted to take two actions:

(a)   To deviate from the right of way sufficiently to bypass the obstruction. (Lord Mansfield, Taylor v. Whitehead (1971) 2 Doug KB 745)

(b)   To remove *only* so much of the obstruction as is required to enable the user(s) to 'pass and repass', and this can only be done if the user(s) are actually in passage. It is not permitted to deliberately set out to specifically remove an obstacle alone. (HA 1980. S.333) and Dimes v. Petley (1850) 15 QB 276)

A reponsible rider will naturally, if possible, make the removed obstruction temporarily 'stockproof' again; reporting this action to the landowner saying you have done your best but suggesting he ought to go out at once to inspect it, has been known to produce better conditions (a gate, for example) especially if repeated several more times. This also applies to a derelict, virtually unopenable gate which may be equally unclosable. The unclosed gate must be reported too, with the reason, as a neighbourly act! However, if temporary measures fail, or are violently rejected, one must try other means.

Further action in regard to obstruction or nuisance

Every example of obstruction or nuisance should be reported, and as soon as possible, to the highway authority. It is no use thinking that someone else should do this, for even if it has been reported before, the continued presence of the problem means that effective action has petered out through apathy and/or a determined refusal of the landowner to deal with it – and all concerned are only too happy to let sleeping dogs lie. The Highway Authority may have inspected the route and be aware of an obstruction, but will take no action unless a member of the public officially reports it – again and again if necessary.

The simple solution is to specify the problem directly to the County Council, with a copy to the Parish Council, and also to the District Council if that has accepted those powers set out earlier in this section. If reporting the offence is going to complicate personal relations between neighbours, then refer the problem to a local or county organization such as a bridleways association or the ramblers association, and ask for assistance.

Keep copies of all correspondence in case it is needed later to prove a point, or the exact lapse of time between your complaint and a continuing lack of any result. If possible, take photographs as evidence, particularly of growing crops sown over a route, giving the date on the back. Try to get other witnesses to complain as well, if possible.

In the event of a really unreasonable delay in the removal of an obstruction, two steps can be taken. One is against the Highway Authority, by complaining to the local ombudsman on the grounds of mal-administration; this can only be done through a county councillor, and the very fact of applying to your councillor may produce the required result anyway. The procedure for applying to the ombudsman is too long to insert here, but is readily available from many sources. Secondly, a member of the public (or a society) can institute a private prosecution against an offender by 'laying an information' before a magistrate under HA 1980. S.137. This is a fairly simple operation, but should not be undertaken without either taking legal advice, or else carefully reading the instructions set out in the book *Rights of Way* by P. Clayden and J. Trevelyan mentioned previously (and in the Bibliography) in order to carry out a 'do-it-yourself' operation.

Two useful legal definitions to remember are as follows:

(i)   'It is perfectly clear that anything which substantially prevents the public from having free access over the whole of the highway which is not purely temporary in nature is an unlawful obstruction'. (L.C.J. Parker, Seekings v. Clarke (1961) 59 LGR 268)

(ii)   'A nuisance to a way is that which prevents the convenient use of the way by passengers'. (Mr J. Byles, R. v. Matthias (1861) 2 F & F 570)

Measures to improve rights of way

Highway authorities can: Signpost and waymark. Provide wardens. Level or alter levels. Drain. Bridge or maintain bridging. Provide gates to bypass cattlegrids. (HA 1980. Sections 6 to 102)

Closure or diversion of rights of way

Closures can be performed under three headings:

(i)   Magistrates court

(ii)   Highway authorities

(iii)   Planning authorities

The closure of vehicular roads (including byways) can only be made by the application of the appropriate authority (usually the County Council) to do so on the grounds that the route 'is unnecessary'. (HA 1980. S.116). An individual who wishes to avail himself of this must do so via the CC. (HA 1980. S.117)

The Highway Authority itself may apply for a diversion either on its own behalf, or for another individual, under the grounds of 'expediency'. The old law regarding the convenience of the user has now gone, and the interest of the owner is the first consideration under the HA 1980. S.119. However, the new path or way must 'not be substantially less convenient' and regard must be paid to the effect on the public enjoyment of the path as a whole, and on other rights of way. (HA 1980. S.119)

Under the TCPA 1971 S.210 provision is made for 'the provision of an alternative highway' – when a bridleway is to be stopped up.

Again, all these orders must be advertised in advance. N.B. All riders should look out for their publication in local papers.

Protecting byways and bridleways

A single rider can effect appreciable results in and around his/her own parish, but a lone voice calling in the wilderness seldom produces considerable action or continuing results. A pressure group of individuals, or an amalgamated body of similar groups, working together in a specified area such as a parish, district or county, is very much more likely to gain attention; their members are, after all, ratepayers and voters, and as such entitled to be taken into account.

A very small band of devoted enthusiasts is enough to get a growing Byways/Bridleways Association into active life; originally perhaps to cover only a few parishes, an area, or maybe all the parishes in a District

Authority. Local riders, after all, are the only people who can accurately identify and report their local problems whatever category that problem may fall into.

Later, with vision and good fortune, it may transpire that the ideal neighbouring groups co-operating together will ensure the coverage of every byway and bridleway in every parish in every district in the county. Who can tell, and why not?

The proposed group, club or association will need a name. Generally speaking, people will work for something they can identify with: a county name, a district name, a local beauty spot, a riding club, etc. It may be strategic to have the word 'bridleway' or 'byway and bridleway' incorporated in the title, but it is not essential. If, in due course, various groups amalgamate or affiliate they can adopt an 'umbrella' title such as 'The X County Byways and Bridleways Association', and (if smaller branches wish to keep their own individuality) refer to themselves as 'The . . . Branch' of the 'X' Association, in official correspondence.

It is a point that, while small is beautiful in regard to caring for rights of way at a grassroots level, a larger and more comprehensive group carries more weight in the County/District corridors of power. But small is quite in order to start out with, or work under.

A new group must have a reason for existence – that is, a few simple aims which are likely to appeal to possible supporters. For example:

(i)   To preserve and protect the registered byways/bridleways in . . . (whatever area is to be covered.)

(ii)   To ensure these byways/bridleways are correctly defined on the Definitive Map.

(iii)   To locate 'lost' byways/bridleways where possible, or negotiate other alternative routes.

(iv)   To circulate relevant legal information and other news among its members.

(v)   To liaise with the relevant Highway Authorities, and encourage them to carry out their statutory duties.

(vi)   To liaise and co-operate with other societies having similar aims.

(vii)   To promote good relations with landowners and/or farmers.

(viii) To act for members in an official capacity when necessary.

The most important achievement of this sort of organization is to take personal conflict out of rights of way. Information sent confidentially to the secretary of the group can be forwarded impersonally on behalf of that organization to the relevant person or authority concerned, so that no neighbours or personalities become involved.

Whatever sort of group, club, society or association is envisaged, large or small, it must have a degree of organization or it will lose credibility, suffer lack of communication and, thereafter, fall into internal dissent. A very simple constitution can lay down the few basic rules which must be adhered to, and sufficient finance to keep the project viable is another matter to take into consideration.

An 'ad hoc' committee can work out in advance some preliminary details of the proposed work that will be involved which can then be produced at an open meeting for interested members of the public; this can save much valuable time at this sort of meeting. Such considerations might include: The duties of the officers. The work to be allocated to members. The lines of communication. The membership fees. The raising of extra finances (fund-raising events, grants, loans, etc.). The allocation of these finances (Postage. Stationery. Printing. Photocopying. Duplicating. Telephone. Travelling Allowances. Insurance. Reference Books. Maps. Clearance Tools). Possible affiliations (Byways and Bridleways Trust. The British Horse Society. The Open Spaces Society. The Ramblers' Association, etc.). Liaison with any larger local organization already in existence (Riding Clubs. Pony Clubs. Driving Clubs. Riding Establishments. Ramblers. Trail Riders. Bridleways Associations. Council for the Preservation of Rural England. British Trust for Conservation Volunteers, etc.). Contact with local and Highway Authorities. Publicity.

In regard to County Council matters, to find out which particular county committee deals with rights of way and/or transport affairs, and also the executive officer in charge of relevant departments (legal, surveyors, planning). Is there a county-run 'Community Council' which co-ordinates and services the various types of volunteer bodies throughout the county? Are grants available from it? Is there a County Sports Council? Where are the county archives kept, for access to tythe maps, enclosure awards, etc.? In which department is the official master copy of the Definitive Map kept?

A small voluntary organization usually needs to have a flexible organization that conforms to its own needs, but it is suggested that there should be a compact nucleus of three committee officers consisting of:

(i)   A chairman

(ii)   A secretary

(iii)   A treasurer

The committee can have the option of co-opting other required members onto the committee, but the above arrangement simplifies the formalities at the open meeting or any annual general meeting since only three officers have to be elected, re-elected or replaced by those members present and voting.

Sources of information

Tracing lost rights of way can be an enthralling occupation, rather like a detective story; the difficulty is not being distracted away down delightful highways and byways other than the particular one you are supposed to be researching.

The task is a vitally important one, all the same; for example, in one Wiltshire parish alone, no less than eight miles of bridleway have been added to the Definitive Map in this way. In other cases, registered footpaths have been discovered to have been originally Public *Roads* from 30 to 40 feet wide. Moreover, the HA 1980. S.32 lays it down that this sort of evidence must be taken into consideration by a court, tribunal or public inquiry concerned with the status of a highway. In most cases proof of the existence of an old highway or right of way will suffice to reinstate it.

For the beginner at the game, the first and easiest approach is to the county archives or record office. Here there will almost certainly be the following:

(i)   Tythe Award maps (plus descriptive apportionments), showing public highways in separate parishes from 1836 onwards.

(ii)   Inclosure Award Maps (with Scripts) showing where new roads were to be made or old ones kept when Common Land was inclosed. However, it often did not show where old roads ran or continued outside that common land. The bulk of these were made about 1845, but there are earlier and later versions; note that not every parish or the whole area of the parish is covered by an Inclosure Award.

(iii)   A large-scale map of the county. These were produced from about 1765, the result of an award from The Royal Society, and are the first accurate County Maps showing existing roads of the time. Different cartographers constructed separate maps for each different county.

(iv)   The first edition OS Maps produced from the early 1800s, though professional surveying started in the last quarter of the previous century. Also held will be a quantity of later maps in various scales, some of them in very large scales indeed.

For future reference, and to save a great deal of time and work later, it is a good idea to buy the relevant section of a copy of the 1st Ed. OS map reproduced by David and Charles (Publishers) Ltd., South Devon House, Newton Abbot, Devon, and mark your findings on it.

The above constitute the first four major sources of information to tackle, and are here followed by other possible sources which can be roughly divided between the chief county museum and its library, or in other departments of the county hall (legal or surveyors, for example) or, again, in the archives.

Maps

Deposited Railway Plans (constructed, or proposed), with Book of Reference. These noted where the line would cut across any right of way, and identified its status.

Deposited Turnpike Plans, with Book of Reference.

Canal Plans. These show proposed bridges to link rights of way, giving status.

Any other old maps of the county, showing roads, turnpikes, etc.

The old national Road Books. (Ogilby, Paterson)

Church Commissioners' Maps.

Estate Maps from the mid 1800s onward.

Estate and Farm Sale Catalogue Plans, and particulars.

Valuation maps prepared under the Finance Act, 1910, with 'Doomsday Book' noting rights of way.

'The Take-over' map prepared under the Local Government Act, 1929, in which the old Rural District Councils mapped out admitted 'maintainable' highways (even the unmetalled ones) prior to handing them over to the county council.

Documents

County Council Roads and Bridges Committee Minutes (earliest to about 1953).

Old Rural District Council Highways Committee Minutes (as above).

Parish Council Meeting Minutes (1895 onwards).

Vestry Meetings (Reports and Accounts of Waywardens and Surveyors of Highways prior to approximately 1835).

Highway District Board Schedules of Roads.

Rural District Council Schedules of Roads.

Canal Board Committee Minutes.

Turnpike Board Committee Minutes.

Railway Board Committee Minutes.

Quarter Sessions Ruling re. highways (presentations for non-maintenance, obstruction, non-clearance of ditches, maintenance of bridges, etc.) up to the end of the 1800s.

Magistrates' Court decisions on highways (closures, diversions).

The relevant 'Victoria' County History.

County or Archaeological Magazines/Journals from the earliest edition for relevant articles on parishes and roads.

Royal Women's Institute Parish Histories.

Any other Parish Histories, or local Family History describing the locality.

This chapter of the book started with 'lore', or fairy stories, so it may well end with the debunking of two cherished Old Wives' Tales. (i) A landowner cannot, himself, close a right of way simply through the lack of use of it. (R.v. Inhabitants of St James, Taunton. Selwyn's Nisi Prius Reports). 'Once a highway, always a highway, unless closed by a recognised legal procedure, nor can the public itself relinquish its rights.' But be warned, and endeavour to keep all RoW open and used lest an application for an extinguishment order on the grounds that the path is unnecessary is put through the council. (ii) It is also not possible to close a path because it is a cul-de-sac (Lord Campbell C.J. Bateman v. Bluck (1852) 18 Q.C. 870). Moreover, if one end of a through path is closed by legal means, the remainder of the path's rights are retained. (Att. Gen. v. Antrobus (1905) 2 Ch 188)

Wildlife and Countryside (Definitive Maps and Statements) Regulations 1983

SCHEDULE 7   Regulation 10(1)

FORM OF APPLICATION FOR MODIFICATION ORDER

Wildlife and Countryside Act 1981

(Title of Definitive Map and Statement)

To: (name of authority)

of: (address of authority)

I/We, (name and applicant) of (address of applicant) hereby apply for an order under section 53(2) of the Wildlife and Countryside Act 1981 modifying the definitive map and statement for the area by

[deleting the (footpath) (bridleway) (byway open to all traffic) from
                             to   ]

[adding the (footpath) (bridleway) (byway open to all traffic) from
                             to   ]

[(upgrading) (downgrading) to a (footpath) (bridleway) (byway open to all traffic) the (footpath) (bridleway) (byway open to all traffic) from
                             to   ]

[(varying) (adding to) the particulars relating to the (footpath) (bridleway) (byway open to all traffic) from   to   by providing that   ]

and shown on the map annexed hereto.

I/We attach copies of the following documentary evidence (including statements of witnesses) in support of this application:

(List of documents)

Dated   19 .   Signed

SCHEDULE 8   Regulation 10(3)

FORM OF NOTICE OF APPLICATION FOR MODIFICATION ORDER

Wildlife and Countryside Act 1981

(Title of Definitive Map and Statement)

To:

of:

Notice is hereby given that on the   19
I/We

of

made application to the (name and address of authority) that the definitive map and statement for the area be modified by

[deleting the (footpath) (bridleway) (byway open to all traffic) from
                             to   ]

[adding the (footpath) (bridleway) (byway open to all traffic) from
                             to   ]

[(upgrading) (downgrading) to a (footpath) (bridleway) (byway open to all traffic) the (footpath) (bridleway) (byway open to all traffic) from
                             to   ]

[(varying) (adding to) the particulars relating to the (footpath) (bridleway) (byway open to all traffic) from   to   by providing that   ].

Dated   19 .   Signed

SCHEDULE 9   Regulation 10(4)

FORM OF CERTIFICATE OF SERVICE OF NOTICE OF APPLICATION FOR MODIFICATION ORDER

Wildlife and Countryside Act 1981

(Title of Definitive Map and Statement)

Certificate of Service of Notice of Application for Modification Order

To: (name and authority)

of: (address of authority)

I/We, (name and applicant) of (address of applicant) hereby certify that the requirements of paragraph 2 of Schedule 14 to the Wildlife and Countryside Act 1981 have been complied with.

Dated   19 .   Signed

Bibliography

Rights of way
Rights of Way: A Guide to Law and Practice by Paul Clayden and John Trevelyan. £5.00 (inc: postage and packing) from either The Open Spaces Society, or The Ramblers' Association. (See address list)

The Encyclopedia of Highway Law and Practice (Sweet & Maxwell Ltd, 11 New Fetter Lane, London EC4P 4EE) Expensive, but probably held by the local reference library. Otherwise, enquire from Sweet and Maxwell. Up to date, and very comprehensive.

Pratt and Mackenzie's *Law of Highways*, 21st Edition. (Butterworth, London) An excellent introduction to general law on highways, but as the last supplement is dated 1967 it contains no Statute Law brought into force since then. Probably held by the local library.

Acts of Parliament, Statutory Instruments and Government Circulars can be obtained from Her Majesty's Stationery Office (HMSO) 49, High Holborn, London WC1V 6HB, or from a local government bookshop whose address will be in a phone book, or simply ordered through a bookseller.

The Story of the King's Highway by S. and B. Webb. From the English Local Government Series, 1922. A well researched book that gives the history of highways and their law from British, Saxon and Roman times through the Middle Ages up to 1920; it provides a far better understanding of modern law on the subject, and the way it works now.

Roads and Tracks of Britain by Christopher Taylor (Dent, 1979). A comprehensive coverage of the development of highways.

Many books written for local historians (*Village Records* by John West, *The Making of the English Landscape* by W.G. Hoskins for example) have sections devoted to the history of highways which indicate sources of information as to their whereabouts, and how to find them.

At least three of the bodies to be found in the list of names and addresses produce regular journals or magazines containing useful and up-to-date information on rights of way. (The Byways and Bridleways Trust, the Ramblers' Association, and the Open Spaces Society. The RA also publishes a bulletin from time to time, called the *Footpath Worker*, dealing with recent court cases, Definitive Map decisions and public path orders.)

General literature
HMSO publishes a series of booklets on the long-distance footpaths; those of interest to rides include: *The Ridgeway Path* by Sean Jennett; *The South Downs Way* by Sean Jennett; *The Pennine Way* by Tom Stephenson.

The Oldest Road: An exploration of the Ridgeway by J.R.L. Anderson (Wildwood House, 1975) is an excellent guide to the Ridgeway.

The British Horse Society publishes *Bed and Breakfast for Horses: Stabling and Grazing*, a very helpful list of places where you might find accommodation for horses en route; also *Where to Ride*, a list of approved riding stables.

Useful addresses

British Horse Society (BHS), British Equestrian Centre, Stoneleigh, Kenilworth, Warwickshire CV32 2LR (0203) 52241.
Aims to further the art of riding and driving and to encourage horse-mastership. The society also seeks to preserve and improve access and rights of way.

British Trust for Conservation Volunteers (BTCV), 36 St Mary St, Wallingford, Oxfordshire CX10 0EQ.
Volunteers carry out practical conservation work, including clearing rights of way. The trust also makes clearing tools available for other groups to do clearance work.

Byways and Bridleways Trust (BBT), 9 Queen Anne's Gate, London SW1.
BBT is a charitable trust which keeps open byways and bridleways. It encourages voluntary work by providing information, both legal and practical, at seminars and in its monthly publication *Byways and Bridleways*.

Council for the Protection of Rural England (CPRE), 4 Hobart Place, London SW1W 0HY.
Includes access to the countryside as one of its main interests.

Countryside Commission, John Dower House, Crescent Place, Cheltenham, Gloucestershire GL50 3RA.
The Countryside Commission works with many organizations and individuals to conserve the natural beauty of the landscape and to provide facilities for access and informal recreation in the countryside of England and Wales.

Endurance Horse and Pony Society of Great Britain (Secretary: Miss M. Gatland, 6 Lundy View, Northam, Bideford, Devon).
Organizes long-distance events.

Forestry Commission, 231 Corsterphine Road, Edinburgh EH12 7AT.
Charged with the production of timber for industry and as supplementary objectives with the provision of recreational facilities . . .

Open Spaces Society, 25a Bell St, Henley-on-Thames, Oxfordshire RG9 2BA (formerly The Commons, Open Spaces and Footpaths Society).
Preservation of common land, village greens, public open spaces, public rights of way and general public access to the countryside. Publishes books and booklets concerning the rights of the public in the countryside.

Ramblers' Association (RA), 1–5 Wandsworth Road, London SW8 2LJ.
Three main aims: to protect footpaths and other rights of way and increase access to open country; to defend outstanding landscape; to encourage people to walk in the countryside.